fruit trees

for the

home gardener

•

other books by allan a. swenson:

•

the gardener's book of berries
plants of the bible
plan your own landscape
wood heat
inflation fighters victory garden
my own herb garden
cultivating carnivorous plants

fruit trees

for the

home

gardener

•

allan a. swenson

Lyons & Burford, publishers

Printed in the United States of America

10   9   8   7   6   5   4   3   2

Design by Kathy Kikkert

Library of Congress Cataloging-in-Publication Data

Swenson, Allan A.
    Fruit trees for the home gardener / Allan A. Swenson.
        p.   cm.
    Includes index.
    ISBN 1-55821-308-2
    1. Fruit-culture.   I. Title.
SB355.S99   1994
634—dc20   94-30550
                                                    CIP

to parker,

katy, and alyssa.

may your lives

be fruitful!

contents

•

acknowledgments

•

During the many years that my family and I raised fruit and berries, we were actually designing our own fruitful landscape. It seemed easy and natural to plant a few fruit trees each year, plus some berry bushes here and there. When it came to putting all those years into my books, I realized how many people had helped me over the hurdles in those years gone by: from my professors at Rutgers University, who suffered through my naïve questions, to nurserymen, who freely offered valuable growing tips. Countless people have played a part in the preparation of this book.

To all of them, especially the dedicated men and women at the fruit breeding and testing stations—and those at the Geneva Experiment Station, in particular—I am indebted. Your efforts have helped make gardens as well as farms across America more bountiful. All of us who enjoy the fruits of our harvests each year appreciate your efforts. May your work in the future prove as abundantly fruitful for generations to come.

introduction

•

Fruit growing isn't as difficult as most people believe. For years, many of us seem to have thought that fruit growing requires lots of space and special talents. That's really not so. With a little extra effort at planting time and some knowledge of pruning, tending, and caring for fruit trees, anyone can enjoy homegrown fruit.

Fruit trees are versatile. They fit well into outdoor landscapes. They provide shade and appealing shapes and forms to grace our homes, gardens, lawns, and property lines. They can grow by themselves or in groups. And they can be successfully grown in many parts of the country.

It seems logical to take advantage of the pleasure, and the bonuses, that fruit trees offer us. Besides having decorative value, they also can reward us with tastier and healthier eating.

Using fruit trees as part of your total landscaping will provide special pleasures. The trees you grow are lovely to look at: food for the soul. The fruits you harvest provide those tasty rewards for the body: fresh fruit, pies, jams, jellies, preserves.

Having traveled every year to visit many parts of America, I have collected the best information from many sources. Each chapter is also based on personal growing experiences, from my youngest days on the farm tending acres of fruit trees to smaller home plantings in recent years.

I hope that you enjoy this guide to tastier living. Each tree you plant, each bush and shrub that bears some fruit, will provide you with a more fruitful gardening experience.

—Allan A. Swenson
Windrows Farm
Kennebunk, Maine
October 1994

1

planning

•

You can enjoy much more

delicious eating when you

landscape with fruit trees.

Actually, you can even *eat*

your own landscape.

Especially on small plots

where space is severely

limited, fruit trees offer

greater versatility than shade

trees or decorative hedges.

. . . .

There is real value in blending different forms, shapes, and leaf patterns as part of a total outdoor scene. When you select furniture for a room, you look for pieces that complement each other but aren't necessarily identical. Some standout accent pieces always lend a special touch. The same is true with outdoor living rooms.

It has been said you can't have your cake and eat it too. But with multipurpose landscaping, you can come close. You'll appreciate the blooms of trees each spring, their fruits in season, and foliage in the fall. What's more, you can taste the difference from a fruitful landscape as you and your family pick and eat the apples, peaches, pears, and plums. You can enjoy your harvests year-round in the forms of pies and cakes, preserves, jams and jellies, canned and frozen fruits and berries, and even wine and brandy.

In parts of Europe, espalier culture of fruit trees has been raised to an art form. Many veteran gardeners have discovered the fun of training fruit trees to distinctive and unusual shapes. You can, too. When you know the secrets, this dramatic technique can provide eye-catching decorative efforts to astound your friends and neighbors. An entire chapter about this espalier growing method is included in this book to enhance your skills.

The great German poet Goethe once observed, "If every man swept in front of his own house, the whole world would be clean."

A famous American nurseryman, Clay Stark Logan of the Stark Brothers Nurseries, added to that thought not long ago.

"Few of us realize how important an abundance of trees is to man and his environment. Right now, we are burning more and more fuel and upsetting more and more the healthful balance of oxygen and carbon dioxide in our atmosphere. For that reason alone, we should have more and more trees because they are nature's principal factories for converting carbon dioxide into oxygen."

Mr. Logan added, "Trees have many unrecognized values. They

add beauty to our homes. Their many distinctive shapes and forms provide variety for more attractive landscape designs. But trees do even more than most people realize. They release moisture that cools the air and washes it. They keep water and wind from carrying away the topsoil that supports all life. They help to keep pollution from washing into our streams."

Trees have monetary value as well. Real-estate agents know that lovely shrubs and beautiful trees add to the dollar resale value of a home. Time after time it has been proven that the well-planted home with the same square footage, number of bedrooms, and facilities outsells the one with few trees and shrubs.

Trees should be one of your first investments as you begin to landscape your home. Once they are well planted, they will grow and set deep, permanent rootholds to reward you for many years. As they grow, you can go about other parts of your annual gardening activities, from arranging beds and borders to planting bulbs, flowers, and vegetables.

As you plan, remember these other benefits of trees. They buffer the wind, especially in winter. They are also nature's best noise barriers. According to the U.S. Department of Agriculture and noise-pollution experts in various urban centers, proper planting can reduce noise pollution by as much as 65 percent.

Even the highway departments are paying more attention to trees and shrubs as a way to muffle roadway noise.

"When we talk about planting a tree today," Mr. Logan observes, "we're not necessarily referring to a giant oak or a large plot of land. Today, no matter what size plot you have, you can grow a tree. That's abundantly true when you consider the advanced state of the plant breeder's art and the work done by pomologists with fruit trees and arborists with shade and nut trees."

With research and new grafting processes, we can enjoy wide new selections of dwarf-size fruit trees. They stand only 6 to 10 feet tall, yet they bear full-size apples, peaches, pears, cherries, and other fruit. Almost any home has room for one of these marvels of nature. You can enjoy several different types or several varieties of one type in the space one large tree would occupy. The smallest ones, such as dwarf peaches, can even succeed in large patio planters, tubs, or barrels.

As you walk around your garden and home grounds, look at the sun that each area receives. Examine the soil to determine how you may improve it. Consider where a peach, apple, or plum tree might prosper. You can set a miniature orchard along a drive or bordering your vegetables. If room is really scarce, pick your pleasure from any of the fruit trees that may fit a special spot.

Multipurpose landscaping with fruit trees is the tastiest way to enjoy the rewards of gardening.

2

the good earth

•

Soil is alive. Even poor
soils have their share of
tiny organisms, helpful
bacteria, and minute
creatures at work
underground.
Depending on its
fertility, every cubic
foot of soil can have
tens of thousands or

even millions of beneficial organisms that have vital functions to perform.

Some devour organic matter, helping to break it down to improve the structure of your garden soil. Others work on soil itself, in cooperation with air and water, to break down minerals and other elements. Creatures like earthworms burrow through soil. As they digest organic material, they leave behind castings, which contain highly valuable nutrients for plant roots.

As organic matter is incorporated into the soil, it improves what is known as the tilth. Soil becomes more crumbly or, as scientists say, friable. Air and water and plant roots can move through soil better when it has good condition.

Some gardens already have rich, deep, fertile topsoil. If yours has, consider yourself lucky. Many homes and developments have been built on former farmland. More often, today, homes have been built on just a light covering of topsoil that's been replaced around buildings after backfilling foundations during construction. Sometimes topsoil has been removed or turned under, and less-desirable subsoil is now on top.

Generally, you'll find variations of soil, including naturally sandy or heavier clay soils, which are common to certain areas throughout the country. Don't fret. Whatever you have can be improved. Nature has been at work for eons building and improving soils.

When you understand and appreciate the basics and know how to make soil come alive, you'll be well on your way to growing more productive, rewarding crops from your land, whatever its original condition.

In its natural state, soil has a *profile*. That won't hold true if you are forced to garden on backfill around a home or building, but soil in natural areas forms in a systematic way. You can look for the profile in a desired planting area by digging down with a spade to reveal a cross-section of earth. If the land hasn't been touched much, you'll find a clearly visible, stratified profile.

The upper level is the topsoil. It is a combination of the broken-down minerals and bits of gravel from the subsoil with the organic matter that has been dropped by living plants and decayed into it.

Below the topsoil is the subsoil. It is usually more gravelly and much lighter in color than topsoil. Below this is the parent material, which may be anything from rocky soil to shales or bedrock, depending on where you live. The profile itself can be shallow, with just a bit of topsoil. Or the profile can be deep, with rich layers of topsoil extending several feet down as in the Great Plains areas.

Soil is formed slowly over tens of thousands of years. If you have good, deep soil, be thankful. But don't despair if your home isn't blessed with good topsoil. All soil can be improved.

It may seem logical to improve a garden area for berries, fruit trees, and even vegetable and flower gardens by purchasing top-soil, but first it pays to have a soil test made on topsoil that you may be thinking of buying, to be sure it has a reasonable fertility and isn't merely fill.

It's best to learn about what type of soil you have around your home. These are the terms that your county agent may use as he or she helps you evaluate your sites and planting areas.

Texture refers to the size of the majority of the particles making up the soil. It ranges from those tiny, almost microscopic clay particles to small stones or gravel.

Clay soils can be stony clay, gravelly or sandy clay, silty, or just plain muddy clay.

Loamy soils may be coarse sandy loams, medium, sandy, fine, silty, or clay loams with an abundance of clay particles in them.

Sandy soils range from gravelly to coarse to medium, fine, and loamy.

Structure of soil is determined by the way in which individual particles are grouped. A good structure lets plant roots, air, and water move freely through it. Loamy and clay soils may have a crumbly structure. Sandy soils have little granulation. Clay soils will compact readily.

For the easiest test to evaluate soil structure, pick up a handful at planting time and make a fist. If it crumbles easily after you have squeezed it in your fist, the soil is probably the desirable sandy loam that will perform quite well. The closer you can improve the structure to a granular feel with clusters of soil that easily shake apart, the better. Organic matter, from peat to compost and humus, will keep you on track in your soil-improvement plan.

Another element should be considered as you go about your soil-improvement program. Three kinds of water are found in any type of soil.

The first is **gravitational water**. In sandy soils, water often drains out too quickly, leaving plants to wilt or perform poorly. In clay soils, gravitational water lingers longer to create soggy spots, with soil pores clogged with water. That will rot roots.

Hygroscopic soil water is that which is bound chemically with soil materials. It is basically unavailable to plants, so it's of no great concern to you.

The most important soil moisture is known as **capillary water**. It is free to leave the soil and enter growing roots. As it does, it carries nourishment into the plants, up through stems or trunks into branches, twigs, and leaves. This water is most available when soil texture and structure are crumbly and loamy, with ample organic matter incorporated into the soil.

There are many simple steps you can take to improve certain conditions rapidly. Other steps will improve soil more slowly, year by year, until it becomes fertile and capable of producing better results than you thought possible.

Compost is one of the most useful materials to improve even good soils. And you can make it right in your own backyard. Some people believe compost is something used only by organic gardeners, but for ages farmers have relied on manure and other organic matter long before chemical fertilizers were widely available.

Back on my original family farm in New Jersey, we also had compost piles working. I still rely on them. They provide that extra boost for many crops, from tomatoes to squash, and help get new fruit trees off to a sturdy start.

You can make compost easily and cheaply. All you need is a small spot to pile organic materials while they decompose into humus. Or you can speed up the process.

layering compost

There are two basic methods of making compost. Simple layering is easier to do, but it will take longer for decomposition to work. Pick any convenient spot on which to pile organic matter. A spot out of sight is best, since a compost pile certainly isn't the most attractive part of a garden.

Pile old grass clippings, fallen leaves, and other organic materials from the garden—pruned softwood branches, debris from thinned plants—into a heap. Take about 4 to 6 inches of this type of material, then a layer of soil about an inch thick. You can spread a pound of lime on the pile and a few inches of manure, if it is available.

If you don't have access to manure, you can spread a few cups of balanced garden fertilizer on the pile. Then add more layers of raked leaves, more clippings from the lawn, and organic *vegetable* debris from the kitchen table; lettuce or cabbage leaves are ideal. Don't use animal fats or bones; they will encourage neighboring pets or other animals to dig into the pile.

Avoid using any diseased leaves. You can use weeds because the heat generated by the decaying vegetation will effectively sterilize most weed seeds.

In this layering process, the anaerobic bacteria will cause the decomposition. They work without the presence of air, but they do their work more slowly than do aerobic bacteria. Always leave a depression in the center of the compost pile. If you don't have rain regularly, keep the pile moist by sprinkling periodically with a hose. This moisture helps the rotting process.

Layering can be done right around your fruit trees. It takes time, but this practice has many benefits. Mulch layering—the simple, convenient process of spreading leaves, straw, grass clippings, and similar materials around your fruit trees—serves to smother weeds, retain soil moisture, and keep soil cool in hot weather. In addition, the mulch gradually releases small quantities of nutrients into the soil as it decays slowly. Plus, it's a great way of disposing of leaves in the fall and grass clippings and plant prunings during the growing season, especially now that many towns ban the burning of leaves and brush. It takes time and money to get lawn trash bags and haul these materials away. You can even ask neighbors for their extra leaves and clippings for your mulching and composting. If they don't want these materials, you both win.

indore method

The other compost method, known as the Indore method, gives you faster results. It is based on the program developed in England many, many years ago by Sir Albert Howard, the father of modern organic gardening. You don't have to be an organic gardener to follow it.

The Indore method has been revised in several ways over the years. All the variations involve turning the compost material periodically so that the faster-acting aerobic bacteria can decompose the material quickly. They work best in the presence of air. You can do the turning by pitchfork, by spade, or mechanically. By placing compost material into bins with perforated sides, or providing wire frames through which air can move more easily, you will encourage this speedier decomposition.

In the accompanying drawings, you see two of the easiest ways to build a simple backyard compost pile. In the first, tiles or cinder blocks are arranged to provide a three-sided bin in which you can pile all types of organic matter. Then, once or twice a week—or more often if you have time—turn the contents. Meanwhile, add water so the anaerobic bacteria can work, too.

Adding manure from cows, sheep, horses, or poultry incorporates nitrogen and small amounts of other nutrients. That's the preferred method of organic gardeners.

You can also add several cupfuls of 5–10–5 or 10–10–10 commercial fertilizer to help speed up the decay and add those extra nutrients in the finished compost.

By following this regular aerating method, you'll be able to get finished compost within two to three weeks if moisture is adequate and the weather is warm. All types of compost activity slow down in dry or cold weather.

The second easy way to establish a compost pile is to use a section of snow fence or wire fencing and set up a sizable round "bin" in which you can accumulate organic material.

hole composting

From parts of Europe where topsoil is sparse and poor, veteran fruit growers brought another soil-improvement technique to America. They knew how to improve soil for fruit trees, grapevines, and other berry-fruit plants simply in holes in the ground.

Consider the spots where you want to plant your trees or bushes. Do they have sufficient good sun, but soil that isn't too promising? Then dig into the ground. Make a hole at least twice the size of the normal spread of the roots of your intended plant in the fall, before you plant.

After you remove the soil, begin placing leaves, manure, and peat moss into the hole in equal, composted amounts. Add grass clippings and kitchen refuse. Add fertilizer, about a cup or two, depending on the size of the hole. Add an inch or so of topsoil to press down the lighter leaves and grass.

Use a spading fork or spade to turn the material periodically. Keep it moist, of course.

If the soil you have removed is rocky but has a fair amount of organic matter and seems reasonably fertile, screen out or pick out rocks and other debris and save the soil to mix into the hole with the compost material.

If you have compost in a pit, you won't have unsightly piles around your yard. Aeration isn't perfect, but you'll be able to see how material rots down into the hole. This porous, organically enriched base is excellent to encourage root penetration and provide better drainage and moisture-holding capacity when you do the actual planting the following year.

One area of our garden in New Jersey some years ago had exceedingly poor topsoil and even worse subsoil. Much of it seemed typical Jersey red-shale soil. To improve the entire area quickly would have involved extensive work. So I tested this compost-hole system. It provided a wonderfully enriched base for a row of blackberry bushes. The next year, I made more holes. For several years I continued to improve the area, several compost holes at a time. By the end of four years, the entire berry area was thriving.

During each year, I also mulched with as much straw, old hay,

. . . .

or leaves from fall raking as possible, up to 6 inches deep along rows and around bushes.

green manure

Plan ahead for fruit trees and berry bushes. A "green manure" crop of winter rye, clover, or similar plants will set deep roots to open the soil for a year before you plant that berry patch, grape arbor, or grouping of fruit trees. Legumes are best. Clovers offer a unique benefit: They afix nitrogen from the air onto their root nodules. When you dig under or till beneath these legume green manures, they release nitrogen freely into the soil and this will benefit your future fruit crops.

Soybeans and snap beans or limas work well. They take little space and, being legumes, they also help improve the soil.

If you decided to set aside an area and improve it for fruit trees, here are some basic pointers. Deep-till the sod 8 to 18 inches deep. If there is no sod, you can start by spreading leaves, grass clippings, or similar material on the surface. When manure is available, spread a 1- or 2-inch layer on the ground. Dig or till it under, working it into the soil.

After the seedbed is raked smooth or tilled evenly, plant your winter cover crop of green manure. Rye is fine. It roots well and will open the soil for spring tilling just before you set your fruit-tree hedge.

If your soil is respectably fertile, and you don't choose to plant green manure, you can prepare the soil in the fall or just before spring planting. You'll note in Chapter 3, Basic Planting Guidelines, and in chapters on specific fruits that some fruits do best when planted in spring; others prefer fall planting. The tender fruit crops, peaches and their relatives in particular, do best when spring-planted.

If you dig or till the selected site in the fall but will wait until spring to plant, spread some fertilizer on the surface in the fall. One pound of 10–10–10 or 10–6–4 per 20 square feet will work into the soil over winter as moisture spreads through the soil.

Most of it will be there when needed at spring planting time, although some will be used to help organic material in the soil decompose. A minor amount is lost, of course, through leaching, especially in sandier soils.

Sandy soils tend to dry out. Many areas, especially the coastal and piedmont regions of the eastern states, have sandy soils. These don't hold moisture well. Neither do the sandy soils of the Southwest. In dry summers, shallow-rooted trees and bushes may suffer badly in sandy soil. Fortunately, there are several easy ways to improve these soils quickly.

Organic matter is the key. You can use fertilizer, compost, or peat moss, which is available from garden centers everywhere. Peat is one of the most versatile products to improve soils, especially sandy types. The best buys are the 6-cubic-foot bales.

Mix a bushel of peat moss to every estimated 2 bushels of sandy soil. Work it in well. Then, after planting, apply about 2 inches of peat moss to the surface as mulch. It will retard evaporation and smother weeds so they don't pull moisture from the soil to rob your plants of that vital element.

In soggier soils, those composed of large amounts of silt and clay particles, plants have another problem. Most trees and berry bushes can't stand wet feet. That's understandable when you realize that plant roots require air to breathe. Without air movement and adequate transfer of nutrients as well as the ability of tiny feeding roots to penetrate soils, plants won't prosper.

Clay soils in dry weather often form hardpans—tight, hard layers, often below the surface—that thwart root penetration. Sometimes you can see this problem on the surface as soil cracks in dry, hot weather. Even these soils, which may exist on just a portion of your property, usually a lower-lying area, can be improved in texture and quality. Here again, organic matter, and especially peat, plays an important role.

Peat moss can be mixed into clay-type soils. But don't do it when they are wet. Wait until they are somewhat dried, so digging or tilling won't compound the problem by forming cloddy clumps. Mixing sand and peat into clay soils is an excellent practice. Use a shovelful of sand with four to five similar amounts of peat moss for 2 to 4 square feet, if soil is heavy clay. Spread the mixture on the surface and dig or till it in. After the first rain, check to determine how much you have improved drainage. If water puddles remain, continue the soil-improvement process. You may need to do this several years in a row to thoroughly improve the area as your plants are growing.

Composted humus, sand on the surface as mulch, and manure also can be spread on clay soils. Each year you'll see improvement as you incorporate organic matter into the ground. Soggy soils are more difficult to improve than sandy ones, but nature will work wonders with your help. As you improve soils, you'll notice that they physically come alive. To prove this fact to yourself, dig a shovelful of soil near a compost pile or an area that has been well mulched. You'll find little creatures—especially earthworms—at work. It has been said that where you find many earthworms, soil is healthy.

Entire books have been written about soil. This chapter is meant as a primer. The good earth may be ready and waiting your planting of these fruitful trees and bushes now. If not, heed the hints of this chapter to improve it.

3

basic planting guidelines

•

Here's a simple, down-
to-earth checklist for
selecting, planting, and
tending fruit trees. It's
brief and to the point.
Other details and
instructions are
provided in chapters on
each fruit. But for easy

reference, this checklist will be helpful. I owe a debt to the fine people at the New York State Fruit Testing Cooperative for making me rethink in briefer terms at times. My thanks to them for this suggestion, which is based on their exceptional knowledge of fruit planting.

1. Everything begins in the soil. Most fruit trees thrive best in deep, well-drained, and friable (crumbly) soils. Pears and plums will do well in heavy soils, but peaches and cherries prefer a lighter soil, a sandy loam.

2. Age of plants is important. The youngest available usually transplant best and are the least expensive. One-year peaches and sweet cherries are most satisfactory. You should order one- or two-year-old trees of apples, pears, and plums. Don't waste money on older trees.

3. Planting time varies for types. Fall is best for sweet and sour cherries, except in cold areas. Apricots, nectarines, peaches, and plums should always be planted in spring. Apples, pears, grapes, and other small fruits can be planted in spring or fall, but most experts recommend spring. If you select spring, do it early so plants get a good start and have extra growing time during good weather.

4. Selecting the right site is important. Plant where you like for eye appeal, convenience, and other personal considerations, provided the soil is good. If not, improve it. But avoid frost pockets—low areas where frost settles—and be sure your site is blessed with ample sun.

5. Pollination is necessary, naturally. Without it, fruit set is reduced or doesn't occur. It is good insurance to have at least two compatible varieties that pollinate each other in the same vicinity. Apples, apricots, nuts, nectarines, peaches, and sour cherries are self-fruitful, but pears usually need a nearby pollinator to set full crops.

6. Variety selection is up to you. However, look over catalogs carefully. Some old-time and new varieties offer special advantages, from great taste to disease resistance. Some are all-purpose; others may be best for either freezing or fresh use, but not good for both.

7. Consider multiple values. Most fruit trees can be used as ornamentals while they produce their bonuses for your table or freezer.

You can enjoy fruit trees as specimens for blooming spring color, summer or fall fruit, and foliage display. Ornamental crab apples fit well in many spots, especially the double-flowering varieties. Nut trees, too, can provide shade and pleasing perspectives, as well as their tasty crops.

8. Bear with your trees and shrubs. They will bear well for you when you plant and tend them properly. Learn what to expect and when. Small fruits begin bearing within two to three years, depending on when you plant them and on the growing conditions those first years. Peaches take three to four years before they begin rewarding you with fruit. Plums and cherries take five before they reach productive maturity. Apples and pears may require five to eight years, depending on the variety.

Dwarf fruit trees usually bear several years earlier than standard-rootstock trees. Remember, to stretch your harvest season, select early-, mid-, and late-bearing varieties. Handy charts on bearing age, productive capacity, and other helpful information are included in the appendices for your convenience. Reading fruit nursery mail-order catalogs will also help you select the best early-, mid-, and late-bearing varieties.

9. Planting is easy, but don't rush through it. Open your plants when they arrive. If you can't plant immediately, heel them in so roots are tucked safely beneath moist soil in a shady spot. If roots have dried, soak them in a pail of one cup compost per one

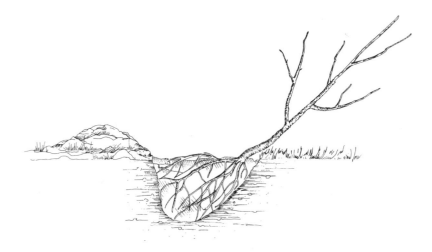

If you can't plant trees when they arrive, heel them into the ground in a shady spot with roots beneath moist soil until you can plant them where they belong.

gallon of water as a slurry. During planting, always keep roots from drying in the sun.

Be sure to dig the hole large enough to give roots space to spread naturally. A Rototiller is handy for digging holes easily. Restricted planting slows growth and may delay your joyous harvest by a year or more. Poor planting can cost you a tree.

Before planting, prune damaged parts and broken root tips. Pack soil firmly. Water well. Standard trees should be set slightly deeper than they grow in the nurseries they came from. Dwarf trees should have graft unions at least 1 or 2 inches *above* the soil. The graft union is indicated by a slight swelling and change in bark color or a slight bend in the trunk near the root. If a middle stem piece has been used for semidwarfing the tree, it will be seen clearly about 12 inches above the root. See Chapters 5 through 10 for details on each fruit and nut in this book.

10. After proper planting, pruning is the single most important factor in producing an abundance of fruit. It stimulates

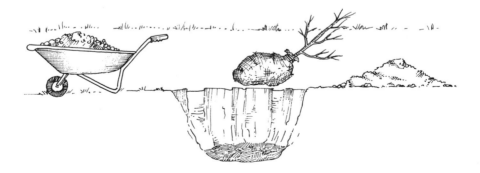

Dig the hole large enough to accommodate the full spread of fruit tree roots, which will insure proper planting and get your tree off to a strong start.

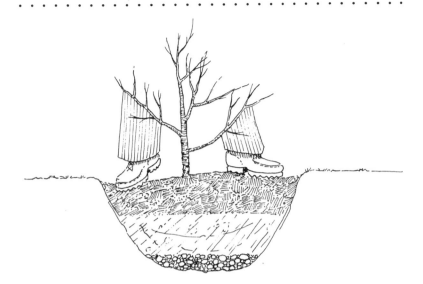

Pack soil well after planting to eliminate air pockets.

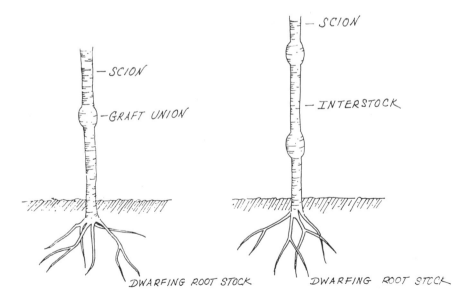

Graft unions are the slight swelling and change of bark color or slight bend in the trunk. Be sure you don't cut off or bury these graft unions.

Stake young trees and use pieces of old garden hose to prevent wire from damaging bark on young trees. Water newly planted trees every few days after planting to encourage new roots to form and provide the sapling with adequate moisture to grow properly.

the growth of shoots, branches, and canes, which results in the new fruiting wood that bears your expected bounty. Read carefully the details for each type of tree. The better you prune, the more success you'll have with fruit plants.

Simply cut tops of new young trees back about one-half their length. Leave two or three well-spaced branches and, except with peaches and their relatives, a leader. Peach, apricot, and nectarine trees have rounded growth patterns. Remove narrow crotches, those that form an angle with the trunk of less than 45 degrees. Make pruning cuts to an outside bud so new branches grow out, not into the center of trees.

11. Mulch facilitates good gardening. Collect and compost old leaves, grass clippings, straw, and similar organic materials. Use them as mulch, or, if composted, use compost as mulch. Mulch prevents moisture from evaporating, smothers weeds, keeps fruit bushes and trees tidier, and adds micronutrients to benefit their growth.

*Use "hardware cloth" wire around young trees to prevent mice from damaging
trunks, especially during winter.*

12. Feed your plants if you expect them to feed you. Nitrogen
is the most important element, but a balance of all essential nutrients
is important. Trees can do well on good soil by themselves, but
for the most abundant crops, year after year, you must put back
into the soil what your growing crops take out. See the sections
on fertilizing in the chapters on specific fruits and nuts for details
and amounts.

13. Insects and diseases can thwart your best efforts to grow
fruit trees and shrubs. Rodents can girdle young trees. Wire mesh

around saplings keeps them away. So do poisons, but use only those that won't harm pets or children.

Resistance to disease has been built into improved varieties by plant breeders and most fruit-tree nurseries now feature these varieties.

New, improved pesticides are safer to use and can help you conquer even the most stubborn problems. Play it safe and always double-check the manufacturer's directions. Be careful while mixing and applying. Always keep chemicals away from youngsters and pets.

14. Know how to tell when fruit is ripe and ready. Details are included in the chapters on individual fruits.

4

general pruning pointers

•

Pruning is one of the

most important aids to

peak fruit production.

Begin training a young

fruit tree the day you

plant it so that it will

develop strong branches

and good form for heavy

fruit production.

pruning pointers

Many gardeners—even veterans—overlook the simple practice of pruning. Perhaps they feel guilty about cutting off those happily growing branches. With fruit trees (and also berry bushes), pruning must be done each year. It not only encourages greater blooming but also produces tastier, better fruit in greater abundance.

In each of the fruit-tree chapters, you'll find easy-to-follow diagrams that show you how to prune your trees from year to year. If you wish to create distinctive designs, follow the tips for espalier training of trees and shrubs. More commonly, you'll want to prune to keep your trees shaped gracefully and allow them to thrive within their allotted space.

Since individual trees vary and different varieties naturally assume somewhat different shapes, these pruning tips are basic. You can modify them as trees get older. One or two branches that interfere with a desired view, block out other plants, rub a building, or otherwise cause problems can be removed, of course, even if cutting them doesn't fit the rules of proper pruning.

If they are not pruned, most fruit trees develop an umbrella shape. This shape is not desirable because outer leaves shade inner parts of the tree, and you get less fruit. Umbrella trees also have many weak limb crotches. They may break apart in storms or when they are heavy with fruit.

Proper training while the tree is young, plus regular pruning later, produces a strong, spreading, open-centered crown that lets light into the tree. It is important to let the sun shine in.

Fruit trees that come from reliable nurseries usually have many more branches than they need. About 75 percent of the tree's roots are destroyed when it is dug from the nursery. This reduced root system will adequately support only a correspondingly reduced number of branches. That means, you must remove many of the branches to compensate for root loss.

To begin training apples and pears, remove all side branches for 2 to 3 feet up the trunk. The first branch at this level that forms an angle of 45 to 90 degrees with the trunk should be left on.

For greater crotch strength, all the major side branches should make angles of about 45 to 60 degrees with the trunk. Limbs that make smaller angles develop weak crotches because the limbs and trunk become pressed together as they grow. Scaffold branches are the basic structural branches of trees.

After you choose the lowest scaffold branch, select four to six other wide-crotch-angle branches spaced 8 to 12 inches apart in a spiral up the trunk. Keep these and remove all the others. Don't keep a branch that is directly above another. It will shade the lower branch.

Then cut each scaffold branch back by one-third its length. Finally, cut back the leader—the top extension of the trunk—so that it extends slightly above the highest point of the side branches.

Train smaller trees such as dwarf apples, plums, and cherries in about the same way. However, the four to six scaffold branches can be closer together and closer to the ground.

Even if you planted fruit trees a few years ago, there is still time to train them by using these pruning methods. The best pruning time is winter, but you can also prune in other seasons to remove excess branches and achieve the desired shape and growth pattern.

If double leaders have developed at the top of the tree, remove one of them. Prune out any water sprouts, those vigorous, upward-growing shoots rising from the trunk or scaffold limbs.

Next, remove suckers, the shoots rising from the base of the trunk. Neither water sprouts nor suckers perform any useful service.

Remove one of any two branches that conflict or rub together. Also prune away any dead branches, all branches with weak crotch angles, and any branches that grow toward and shade the tree's center. After a number of years, you may also wish to cut out the leader to limit the tree's height.

Here are the most important points for proper pruning:

Make sure to use well-sharpened tools. Smooth, clean cuts can be made only with sharp tools. Clean cuts heal more quickly than ragged ones. Decay often starts in ragged cuts and may then enter the main trunk to weaken the entire tree structure. Cut branches flush with the trunk of the tree. Don't leave stubs. They heal slowly and invite disease.

Place the cutting blade of your shears below or at the side of the crotch. Never place it in the crotch of the tree. *Do* and *don't* illustrations show the right and wrong way.

If you prune regularly, you will find it easier to remove small branches and suckers rather than having to saw away larger limbs.

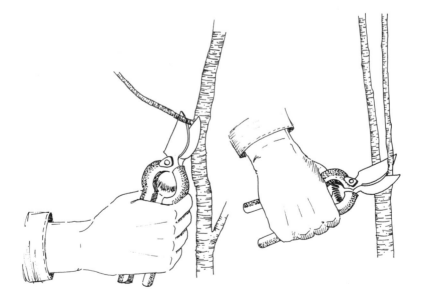

There is a right and wrong way to prune. The version on the left is correct. Position shears to remove the unwanted branch. On the right, the wrong way: this leaves too long a shoot that can lead to new, useless growth.

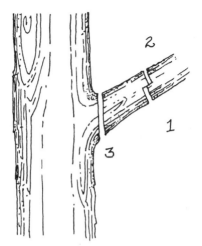

To remove a heavy limb, first (1), make a cut below. Then (2), cut from the top to remove the limb. Finally (3), saw the remaining stub off. This system prevents the weight of a heavy limb from tearing back down the tree trunk as it falls.

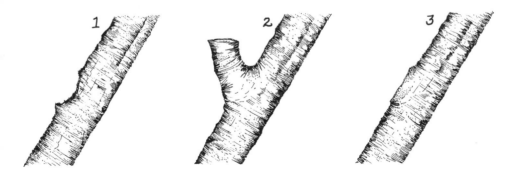

When you remove medium-size branches, follow this guide. (1) shows a cut too close into a main limb. (2) shows a cut too far away with excess stump left. (3) is how the cut should look when completed properly.

If you must remove a large branch or limb, here's how to avoid tearing the trunk bark:

Make a 2-inch-deep cut in the bottom of the limb, about 6 inches from the base. Next cut down into the limb about 8 to 10 inches from the trunk. When the limb falls, the undercut prevents tearing of the bark down along the trunk itself. Finally, use a sharp saw to remove the stub as flush to the tree as possible without cutting into the trunk itself.

When you must remove large limbs that have become diseased, damaged, or broken by storms, remove them cleanly. Any wound from a branch or limb more than 2 inches in diameter should be painted with a standard tree-wound paint. You can get such paint under several brand names in hardware stores, garden centers, and garden departments of some chain stores. Mail-order firms also sell it.

With large cuts, it helps to finish your pruning as a professional tree surgeon would, leaving an elliptical shape. This lets water drain away, rather than catch in a rough or ragged spot where fungus or other problems can start. Use a sharp knife or chisel and shape the wound from the removed limb as shown in the illustration. It will heal more quickly and more surely than a sloppy wound and will prevent problems. Again, coat or paint these larger wounds with tree-wound paint.

5

apples

•

Once upon a time, just

about every home had

an apple tree or two.

Today, largely because

of suburban sprawl,

thousands of acres of

small apple orchards

are gone. The bulk of

our apple crop is

produced in

commercial orchards, which concentrate on high-yielding, easy-to-harvest, mostly red varieties that fare well in shipping and maintain color—but at the expense of great flavor. Gone from supermarket shelves are many of the tastiest, juiciest, best pie-making and baking varieties.

Fortunately, renewed interest in home vegetable gardening and natural foods has rekindled interest in home fruit growing. Luckily, many of the best among the old-time favorite varieties are still retained by some nurseries. They are available today to provide far more flavorful apples than you can buy in stores. You can grow Northern Spy and Winesap or even such exotic delights as Winter Banana right in your own backyard.

Apples offer multi-season beauty just about anywhere you want them. When apple-blossom time arrives, they perfume the spring air. Their delicate pastel pink blooms are harbingers of spring as much as the daffodils blooming beneath them.

Dwarf and semidwarf rootstocks make it possible to fit several trees into the same growing room that a standard tree requires. Dwarfing rootstocks limit tree size to low-growth smaller trees. Semidwarf rootstocks limit tree size to about half the size that a normal tree would grow. They can be planted as close as six to eight feet apart, compared to the 35- or 40-foot spacing required by a standard variety. This development more than any other single factor has led to the apple tree's return to home gardens. Their attractive shapes and distinctive growth patterns fit tidily into landscape plans. Combination plantings of several varieties let you enjoy their slightly different blooms in spring and contrasting fruit colors in fall.

True dwarf fruit trees are prolific bearers of full-size fruit. They even have a tendency to overbear that usually derives from the bearing variety. Some folks complain that dwarf trees are somewhat shallow-rooted. With a heavy fruit crop in season, or when

· ·

laden with ice during winters, they may tip and uproot. But these problems can be easily corrected by thinning the fruit and bracing or staking the trees.

Dwarf apple trees are the result of grafting the desired flavorful varieties on special rootstocks developed originally at the East Malling Fruit Research Station in East Malling, England. Over the years, plant breeders have discovered and cultivated different types of dwarfing rootstocks that permit different degrees of dwarfing.

These rootstocks are usually identified by Roman numerals. In recent years, other "dwarf-size-inducing" rootstocks have been used to create these space-saving trees. These include Geneva 65, Budagovsky, Mark, Ottawa, Interstem, Malling-Merton, and others. You may also find the Malling stocks with regular, or Arabic, numbers rather than the Roman-numeral identifications. An understanding of what these rootstocks do, whichever type is used, is helpful in your fruitful landscape planning.

Malling IX (or 9) has been widely used in all parts of the country. It is also used commercially where orchardists wish to contain the size of their trees for ease of spraying and harvesting. This is the best of the fully dwarfing rootstocks. It keeps the apple tree no taller than 8 or 9 feet over a twenty-year period. That's handy. You can easily prune and pick apples from these trees while standing on the ground. Trees on Malling IX stock are useful for very small plots. You can use them on front lawns or as specimens at the corners of your house.

Trees on **Malling VIII** are also dwarf and perform about as well as the IX ones. Some nurseries offer apples on other types of dwarfing rootstock that work as well.

Since these trees take little space, you can plant a hedgerow of them along a driveway or property border. They neatly screen out unwanted views, yet remain easy to trim and tend.

Dwarf trees grace even a small patio and provide tasty fruit.

Malling II is another popular semidwarfing rootstock used by many nurseries to produce smaller apple trees. It is hardy and encourages early and prolific bearing. This rootstock will produce mature trees about 15–18 feet high.

Malling VII is similar and has the advantage of somewhat greater drought resistance. It is more vigorous and hardy than **II**.

Malling I, II, III, IV, V, VI, and **VII** are all dwarfing or semidwarfing rootstocks. However, **VIII** and **IX** are considered the best for producing true dwarf trees.

Some of the earlier Mallings have shown a tendency to develop suckers or make a poor union with some apple varieties, so plant breeders have been working with and introducing other types of dwarfing rootstocks. Many more nurseries now offer them in addition to the earlier Malling stock.

Another method of producing semidwarf trees is grafting. For example, a hardy standard rootstock may be used on which a **Malling VIII** interstock or newer type **interstock** is grafted in the nursery, with the desired bearing variety grafted on top of the **interstock**. Interstock is the piece of dwarf-inducing plant material grafted between the rootstock and desired bearing variety to achieve a smaller tree size.

According to plant breeders, the degree of dwarfing is increased with the length of the interstem used. Other nurseries offer dwarf trees on other, newer dwarfing rootstocks too.

In general, the interstem method of creating smaller trees usually produces trees about one-third to one-half the size of standard fruit trees. Research is continuing on these fronts to produce even more convenient sizes of apple trees.

As you shop for dwarf fruit trees, check with your local nursery or read the mail-order fruit catalogs carefully. That way you'll be certain to get the stock that will produce a tree of the size and shape you want so it fits properly into its desired place in your landscape.

. . . .

Dwarf trees have advantages other than size. They usually begin to bear two or more years earlier than standard-size trees.

You can expect about a bushel of apples from a dwarf tree about the size of a mature, standard peach tree, no more than 8–10 feet tall. Early bearing is appealing, since you can enjoy apples sooner. Dwarf trees have a lifespan of approximately twenty to twenty-five years before they begin to decline in vigor.

Dwarf trees also let you plant several varieties of fruit with different seasons. Some will bear early, others in midseason, and others in late season. That stretches your apple-eating harvest over more months.

If you do have lots of room, of course, you can plant standard trees. Some of these, and dwarf or semidwarf types too, have been grafted with several varieties. As trees begin to bear, you can pick Red Delicious, McIntosh, Yellow Delicious, and others right off the same tree. The grafts of the different varieties by experts have created these 5-in-1 apple-growing wonders. In general, it is better to grow several desired variety trees, since care of a 5-in-1—especially pruning—is a bit tricky.

You will find at the end of this book a list of reliable mail-order nurseries. Some are large, while others are small and specialized. They provide a wider selection of varieties than most local nurseries can supply.

There are more than 2,000 varieties of apples. Many began as chance seedlings. However, only about 100 of these are of commercial or home-garden importance today.

Which varieties you select will depend on your own individual taste, of course. For convenience, here are some of the best for eating fresh, for cooking, and for baking in pies. By the way, homemade applesauce is far more delicious than the jars and cans you buy in stores.

Quinte is very early and hardy. The fruit is medium-size, red with yellow streaks. The flesh is soft, aromatic, tender, and great for dessert.

Prima is early midseason. The tree is moderately vigorous and spreading. The fruit is medium-large with 60 percent dark red color on bright yellow background. The flesh is fine-grained, firm, crisp, and excellent for fresh or cooking use. This variety tends to resist apple scab disease.

McIntosh is popular for home gardens. Trees are hardy and vigorous. The fruit is medium-size, bright red, blushed with carmine strokes. The flesh is firm, crisp, and very juicy. Variations of the old McIntosh have been developed. **Rogers** and **Red McIntosh** are two good ones.

Macoun is a midseason-ripening variety. Trees are upright, hardy, and bear medium-size, dark red-striped fruit. The flesh is semi-firm, crisp, and white, excellent for fresh use.

Spartan is another midseason variety with upright vigorous growth. The fruit is solid dark red, firm, crisp, juicy, and white. This apple is more resistant to preharvest drop than McIntosh.

Cortland ripens in midseason with semifirm, crisp, juicy fruit. It is noted for white flesh that does not brown readily and thus is good for dessert, cooking, and salads.

Priscilla ripens in midseason. Its shape is conical to round, glossy, with white to slightly greenish flesh. It, too, is reportedly nearly immune to scab as well as resistant to fire blight and powdery mildew, so it is easier to care for.

Idared ripens late on upright, very productive, vigorous trees. The fruit is medium to large, bright red with creamy white, firm flesh, good for cooking and eating. It retains quality under storage long after harvest.

Mutsu, a Japanese introduction, is very vigorous and productive. It bears large golden yellow fruit late in the season. The flesh is yellow white, crisp, and is good for many uses. It is a good variety to replace **Golden Delicious** because its leaves are free from russeting and have resistance to fruit-spray injury. It, too, has long storage potential, but it must be grown with other varieties to ensure proper cross-pollination.

Fuji is a juicy, firm, white-flesh apple that dominates apple-growing in the Orient. It has an aromatic sweet taste with crops ripening mid to late October.

Some apples are more susceptible to insect and disease problems than others. Hybridizers have been working on tasty varieties that have built-in genetic disease resistance.

Janafree is unusually resistant to common diseases such as apple scab and cedar rust, and also fights fire blight and mildew. It bears heavy crops and ripens in mid-September.

Liberty is an unusually resistant McIntosh. It is hardy and bears huge crops in late September.

Redfree is an early-ripening disease-resistant apple that is tasty for fresh use and trees bear in August.

For a special flavor, **Criterion** is a combination of **Red Delicious, Yellow Delicious,** and **Winter Banana**. It is excellent fresh, cooked or in pies, and stores well. It ripens in October.

Early-maturing varieties such as **Lodi, Summer Rambo**, and **Grimes Golden** usually are attacked less by insects and disease than are varieties that ripen later. One main reason is that fungus diseases favor warm weather and moisture, which usually occur later in the summer. Other varieties have been developed to beat pest problems by inbred genetic factors. Fruit catalogs usually spotlight varieties with such useful characteristics.

If you love apples, you might consider joining the New York State Fruit Testing Cooperative Association in Geneva, New York. It has a long record for developing, testing, and introducing exceptional new fruit trees and bushes.

As a member, you can buy new test varieties for evaluation in

Golden Delicious apples in home orchards are a tasty treat.
Photo courtesy USDA.

your home garden. You can also get a wider range of apple varieties than you can from most other sources. The association offers stocks of **Burgundy**, a blackish-red apple; **Ozark Gold**, a Golden Delicious type; **Vista Bella**, one of the very earliest red apples; and some of the old-time exotics.

Apple connoisseurs can find **Winter Banana** or **Westfield Seek-No-Further**, **Snow Apple**, **Smokehouse**, **Sheepnose**, **Sops of Wine**, and others in the Miller Nurseries catalog. They specialize in dwarf and semidwarf stock.

If you wish to avoid or cut back on use of pesticides and fungicides, focus on the newer, disease-resistant varieties. Stark Brothers Nurseries lists a fine assortment from **Jonafree** and **Liberty** to **Prima** and **Redfree**.

If you live in northern areas, focus on winter-hardy varieties such as **Arkblack**, **Winesap**, **Granny Smith**, **Yellowgold Delicious**, **Lodi** on **Compspur** stock.

By requesting a selection of free catalogs, you can also locate such great-tasting but strangely named apples as **Chenango Strawberry**, with its long, conical shape; **Esopus Spitzenburg**, with a heady aroma and orange-red color; and **Red Astrachan**, a beautiful early summer apple.

crab apples

Don't overlook the beauty of flowering crab apples in your living landscape. Conventional single-flowering crab apples are hardy and provide profusions of bloom. They reward you with those marvelous bright little apples for making jelly that just can't be duplicated by jelly manufacturers. Decorative double-flowering crab apples offer greater profusions of bloom. They vary in form and size from the shrublike **Sargent** to narrow upright **Pink Spires** and the wide-spreading **Lemoine**. Some are weeping, others vaselike;

still others are more irregular and picturesque.

You can get flowering crab apples with white, pink, or red blooms. They may bear single flowers with five petals or semi-double and double with clusters of petals.

The fruits of flowering crab apples may range from pea-size to multipurpose ones 2 inches in diameter. Their color is generally red, purple, or yellow. If you wish to fit crab apples into your planting scheme, select flowering varieties on the basis of their fruit rather than flower array alone. Flowers are colorful for one week to ten days. Fruits last up to six months unless you pick them for jelly making. They also have the advantage of being excellent food for birds during those long, cold winter months.

Consider the particular crab apple variety's susceptibility to disease, too. **Hopa** is popular and produces large fruit. However, it is most susceptible to scab, a common disease of apples. Scab can be transferred to other apple trees if it becomes established on a susceptible crab-apple variety.

Redbud is one of the best all around. The buds are pink, the flowers white, and the pea-size fruits last all winter. **Adams, Profusion**, and **Red Splendor** are better than **Hopa**. They have reddish foliage and reddish-pink flowers. Their fruits are more colorful, and they are quite resistant to apple scab.

planning for apples

Apples like sun and reasonably fertile, well-drained soil. Once you spot the ideal location where the beautiful, delicate blooms and sweet perfume will waft across your garden, prepare the soil for planting. Dig in deeply and do this job right. A little extra effort at planting time will let your tree set its roots deeply and well for a long, happy life.

Fall is the best time to prepare the soil. Then, when your trees arrive in the spring, you will be prepared to put them in the ground, even if the weather is not yet perfect. That way, you get a jump on planting, before other garden chores press you for time.

In milder areas of the country, where temperatures are seldom below zero, trees may be planted in fall, winter, or early spring; any time the ground is not frozen. The roots of apple trees are more tender than their tops. Therefore, in colder areas, early fall planting is best for apples, pears, sour cherries, and Japanese types of plums.

Fall planting has some advantages over spring planting. Often soil is in better condition. Weather also may be more favorable, as fewer windy days or long wet periods occur in fall than in spring. A fall-planted tree also has time to get a good roothold and be ready for strong spring growth when warm weather arrives. That gives you almost a year's growth advantage toward earlier bearing.

planting tips

Organic matter is valuable for all growing things, whether trees, shrubs, flowers, or vegetables. Plan to mix into the soil whatever organic material you have or can get. Use peat moss or manure, compost or leaf humus. These materials will open heavier soils to let roots, water, and air penetrate better. They will also improve the moisture-holding capacity of sandier soils to avoid drought damage in dry periods.

Manure and compost are usually more readily available in fall than in the spring, the peak sales season for local suppliers. And prices may be lower. You may also be able to get manure from riding stables or farms free for removing it in the fall, rather than pay for manure when everyone wants it in the spring.

Whichever season you prefer to do your planting, remember that fruit trees should be set before the middle of April, while they are still dormant, not yet leafing out. Most trees arrive from nurseries bare-rooted. You can buy container-grown or burlap-balled trees locally, but they usually cost somewhat more.

Young one- or two-year-old plants are the best buy. You can buy older plants, but tests have shown that often they don't begin bearing any sooner because they may experience greater transplanting shock.

You can dig the holes for your trees by hand or prepare the ground by rototilling. I consider a Rototiller the second most important power garden tool next to a lawn mower. It can dig holes for trees, beds for shrubs, and gardens for flowers and vegetables. It can also be used to cultivate and turn under anything from sod to layers of organic matter for improving the soil. You can usually rent them, too.

If your soil is poor, by all means improve it. Details on this vital practice are included in Chapter 2.

Give your trees enough room to grow naturally. Position dwarf apple trees 10 to 12 feet apart each way or 6 to 8 feet apart in rows with 15 feet between the rows. That's ample space to let them mature properly and for you to tend them well.

Place semidwarf apple trees about 20 feet apart each way. Standard trees will need 35 to 40 feet between them to reach their full growing potential without crowding. If you plan to create hedgerow effects, you can plant all sizes 4 to 5 feet closer than these suggested distances. Pruning will be somewhat more complicated, but as property borders and living screens to block out unwanted views, fruitful hedgerows are functional as well as attractive.

Before you plant any tree or bush, consider its size at maturity. Keep trees and shrubs far enough away from buildings and property lines to avoid maintenance problems.

Remember, too, that fruit trees and bushes may require periodic spraying. Your neighbors may object to spray drift on their property, although this is less a problem than it may seem. Proper spraying can keep drift to a minimum.

Dig each hole large enough to accommodate the entire root system without crowding. The hole should be deep enough to allow the tree to be planted at the same depth it grew in the nursery. You can usually see that depth indicated by a different color and texture of wood on the trunk.

While you dig, separate the topsoil from the subsoil. If the soil is good, spread some of the topsoil in the bottom of the hole and spread the roots gently over it. Then sift more topsoil around the roots. Add improved soil that is combined with manure or compost, as indicated in Chapter 2.

If the soil is extremely acidic, mix 1 to 2 pounds of limestone with the soil in the hole at planting time. Some authorities recommend incorporating fresh manure or chemical fertilizer into the soil. Better advice is to add fertilizer later, on top of the ground after planting is completed, so as to avoid damage to tender root hairs.

If you have decided to plant dwarf or semidwarf apple or other fruit trees, be certain to keep the graft union *above* the ground. Look at the illustrations in this chapter. They apply to all dwarf or grafted trees and plants, not just apples.

Continue to fill the hole with soil, tamping it down with your fist or foot to eliminate air pockets. When it is half full, water well. Then fill to the top and tamp again. Leave a saucer-shaped depression with a soil dike 15 to 18 inches around the tree. This helps collect rain to encourage new roots to form. Root development occurs when soil temperature reaches about 45 degrees F.

After the first watering, provide enough water to keep the soil moist at least 6 inches deep, especially during dry periods to get your young tree well started. For winter protection the first year, mound soil slightly around the tree to reduce frost heaving, but keep soil away from the trunk to avoid bark damage.

Mulching with straw, compost, peat, and grass clippings also helps protect the tiny, tender new roots that are forming. But keep mulch away from the trunk to prevent organisms that may be in the mulch from causing decay.

Mice and rabbits like to nibble on newly planted fruit trees, and can girdle and kill trees by chewing off the bark all around the trunk. All other such creatures are also likely to cause trouble.

Use quarter-inch wire hardware cloth wrapped around the trunk 18 inches high. Press it several inches into the ground so burrowing mice can't sneak past. Don't tie it to the trunk. Allow an inch of space, as the illustration indicates, so it doesn't rub against and injure the bark.

fertilizing

Many people know they must fertilize their vegetables in order to produce abundant crops. They realize that houseplants need nutrients too, and often, in their zeal, kill houseplants by overfeeding.

For some peculiar reason, lots of folks I know seem to believe that trees just grow all by themselves. After all, they ask, don't trees grow by themselves in forests and woodlands? That's true enough. But if you want to enjoy the bountiful fruits of apple growing, you must feed your trees so they will return the favor.

After planting, apply a cup of 10–10–10 fertilizer in a circle about 18 inches out from the trunk. Incorporate it into the soil with a cultivator so that water and rain will dissolve it properly.

When trees begin to grow, scatter 1 to 2 pounds of good, balanced garden fertilizer, fairly high in nitrogen, in a circle around each tree each spring. Garden centers usually have balanced fertilizer mixes designed specifically for fruit trees. As tree limbs spread

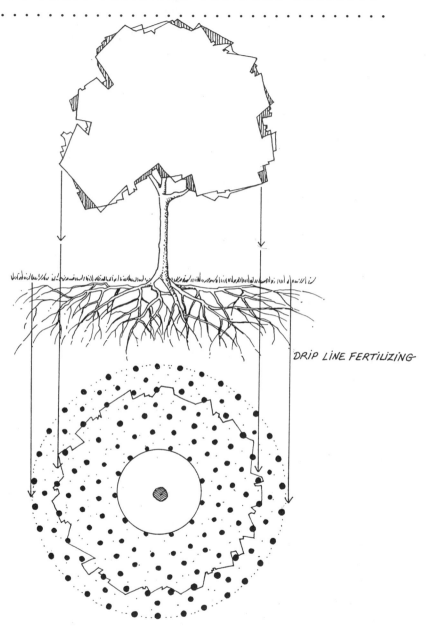

DRIP LINE FERTILIZING

Roots extend much farther underground than most people realize, so you should apply fertilizer in circles out to the "drip line" of the established tree.

out, they indicate how far the root feeding zone of the tree extends. On poorer soils, a supplement during June may be helpful. Here are some good green-thumb rules for feeding apple trees properly:

Too much fertilizer will cause trees to grow too vigorously. Strange as it may seem, that's bad. Excess fertilizer will reduce blossoms and produce small quantities of poor-quality fruit. It is better to supply a minimum quantity of fertilizer each spring and supplement it later if necessary.

For large, well-established trees, it is best not to exceed 5 pounds of complete fertilizer for spring applications. If trees are overvigorous and sprouting sucker shoots, water sprouts, and extra crisscross branches, reduce your application. A tree in proper vigor will produce about 12 inches of terminal growth by the end of July. If the growth is only 2 or 3 inches, your tree is undernourished.

As a supplement to the 1 to 2 pounds of balanced 8–8–8 or 10–10–10 each spring, add a quarter-pound of sodium nitrate or the equivalent from some other nitrogenous fertilizer for each year of the tree's age, up to a maximum of 3 pounds per year.

As you use apple and other fruit trees for part of your total landscape scene, you may prefer some as specimens on lawns. Certain fruit trees—including peach, sour cherry, and plum—grow poorly in sod. Apples can thrive on lawns. However, for all trees in lawns, it does help save time and avoid bruising trunks if you leave a mulch or clean cultivated circle 12 to 24 inches in diameter around each tree. Mulch is preferred because it also retains soil moisture and provides some micronutrients as it decays.

The basic framework of your tree is established during pruning in its first and second seasons' growth. It is best to prune trees in late fall when leaves have fallen, or during mild winter weather. You can see their overall pattern better. Never prune in summer.

One-year to two-year apple and pear trees normally arrive from the nursery as straight, unbranched 4- to 5-foot whips. They hardly look like much. You might think that your hard-earned cash has bought you an ungainly and unsightly tree that can never become what you expected from those lovely color pictures in the catalogs. Take heart—with time and proper care, it will.

At planting time, prune these tall whips to a height of about 3 to 4 feet. Also prune broken or injured roots to a clean cut before planting. During their second year, these trees will produce side branches all along and around the main trunk. They may not look capable of doing that, but if you plant, water, and feed them well, they will indeed begin to take a more substantial-looking shape in future years.

At the end of the first season, remove branches to a height of 24 inches. Trees grow from the top and tips of branches. A given point on a trunk, say 24 inches above the ground, remains at that level. Low branches are not necessary for fruit production, and they interfere with mowing and other work around the trees.

Remove any branches that form a narrow angle with the trunk. Angles of less than about 45 degrees are naturally weaker. They tend to split when boughs are heavy with fruit and can ruin an otherwise fine tree. Limbs that form about 90-degree angles with the main trunk are strongest.

Look at the tip of your tree. Remove one of any two branches that tend to divide the tree into a "Y" shape. Leave only one central leader. If there is damage to the leader, remove it. Trees naturally tend to send up a new leader from one of the topmost branches near the trunk.

If you have bought and planted two-year-old or older trees, prune them according to directions for trees that have completed their first years of growth in your garden. Remove limbs that form weak crotches. Keep only the best branches along the main trunk

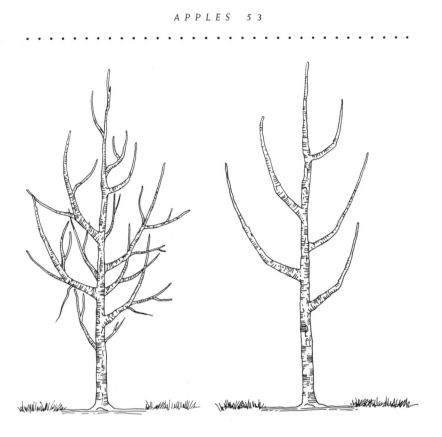

On the left, a young apple or pear tree that has become scraggly and over-branched should be pruned to encourage its best potential growing and bearing shape as on the right.

and a leading branch that is a continuation of the main trunk.

It may seem harsh, but it is best to prune second-year trees back severely, removing about half their growth. That pruning will establish their proper form and framework for years to come.

After the second season, and until your trees begin to bear, only corrective pruning is required—such as removing suckers, water sprouts, winter-damaged branches, or any branch that rubs against another. Don't prune more than necessary during these years. Excess pruning then only encourages long sucker growths in tops of trees. Moderate, careful pruning the third, fourth, and fifth years results in earlier fruiting.

When your tree begins to bear its tasty crop, its limbs will bend with the weight. Don't worry. This natural growing process helps open the tree, spreading its branches and giving it form and balance. Annual growth also will be somewhat reduced, so less pruning will be needed.

In future years, thin out branches that rub together. Leave the strongest and best that establish your tree's shape. Remove water shoots and sucker growth. (These are the long, spindly shoots that sprout tall from the trunk and along limbs. They serve no useful purpose and bear little if any fruit.)

Individual apple-tree varieties differ in growth habits. Adjust your pruning efforts to keep the tree open to air and sun. If storm damage occurs, prune judiciously, removing only the damaged branches so new growth can fill in and rebuild the tree's symmetry.

If you plant hedgerows, remove branches and limbs that grow out in the opposite direction from the row. Keeping apple hedges only 3 feet wide offers a challenge, but they can be kept neatly in line and bearing well for years.

The diagrams in this chapter and in Chapter 4, General Pruning Pointers, will help you take those first cuts. Afterward, prune moderately to maintain the size, shape, and pattern that pleases you and fits your landscaping plan.

Consider pruning a fact of apple-tree life. Fruit wood of a productive tree is continuously weighed down by each year's crops. These limbs never fully regain their height again.

Scaffold branches crowd and depress lower branches. That makes it necessary to continuously remove and thin out some of the other fruit branches. Never fear. New upright growth appears on upper portions of the scaffolds. That's what you want. By cutting out drooping branches and leaving the more upright-growing

Remove water sprouts from branches and trunk and suckers from root areas to help
your tree attain its best growth and eliminate unwanted inner growth.

ones you are letting your tree adjust for wood that must be removed (such as branches that rub others or are simply excess branches that reduce air flow and sunlight). A vigorous tree, well fed and tended, may be twenty to thirty years old, while the fruiting wood created by your regular pruning efforts is only five to ten years old. In effect, pruning lets you keep your tree young and productive.

thinning

Each spring you'll see buds awaken and burst forth in bloom. Each bud is capable of being pollinated to produce an apple. Seldom are they all visited by bees and pollinated. Some years, however, favorable conditions will produce an overset of fruit. That can weigh down your trees branches and break them.

When this happens, you might be tempted to prop up the branches. Usually that action is foolish. Too abundant a set of fruit usually results in smaller, less desirable apples. It is far better to take time every spring to thin your fruit. This simple practice lets the remaining fruit be nourished fully to produce plumper, larger, juicier apples.

Most fruit trees do have a natural drop of newly set fruits because of high winds, because the tree "knows" it cannot supply all fruits with sufficient food and water, or for other natural reasons. Nature planned things that way.

After the natural drop, if the remaining fruits are still too plentiful to mature as well as they should, thin them by hand. An excess is anything more than one fruit for each 6 to 8 inches along a branch. Simply pick off tiny fruits within twenty days after trees have bloomed.

It is especially important to hand-thin on dwarf trees, as they may set far more fruit than they can carry. When they do, you'll find fruits smaller and less tasty at maturity, and your tree may not bloom the next year.

You may find that only scattered limbs on a particular tree need thinning. It's not so big a chore. An hour or less per tree is usually all the time required.

pest control

Insects enjoy eating apples as much as people do. Codling moths, aphids, and other chewing, sucking, and tunneling pests can plague you if you're not prepared to fight them off.

New chemicals are being perfected and introduced, and advances are being made in pest control every year. Some pests are more prevalent in certain parts of the country than in others. Control is important because pests don't damage just a few fruits and leave the remaining ones for you. They can destroy an entire year's crop unless you control them.

Consult Chapter 12, Pest-Control Guidelines, for a basic plan to win your battle with bugs and blights. Be alert for new products that offer even better pest control as they are introduced through garden centers locally. You can beat the bugs when you know how.

Most states have recommended insect-control programs that work well. Consult with your state fruit-growing extension specialist at your state agricultural college and with your local county agricultural extension agents. They have the latest information for your effective approach to insect control.

harvesting

Within a few short years, dwarf trees begin to bear. Standard trees take longer. Some varieties, like **Northern Spy**, may try your patience before they become productive. But when those first fresh, shiny apples ripen, be prepared.

As mentioned, preharvest dropping is natural. You'll find that some varieties fall more readily than others. As your apples seem plump and ripe, check around the trees. It pays to pick the fruit before it drops and bruises. Apples continue to ripen well off the tree and can be stored in a cool part of your basement or garage. Use those with bruises or blemishes first; don't try to keep them. One bad apple really *can* spoil a bushel.

Drops can be used for cider. In fact, now that fruit growing has become so popular again, many hardware stores and national department stores with extensive mail-order catalogs offer presses for apples and other fruit. Instructions for making cider accompany the presses.

Recipes for apple jelly and for pie, strudel, cake, and other delicious delights abound in magazines and cookbooks.

Once you have enjoyed the first few apples from your trees, you should reread this chapter. Improve the soil around your trees. Feed them well. Be sure they have sufficient water as harvesttime approaches. Prune properly every fall and winter. If you follow the simple apple-growing steps, you'll be assured of more and better apples year after year.

6

pears

•

Pears deserve to be
grown much more
widely in home
gardens, especially con-
sidering the new
introductions with
exceptional hardiness
and flavor that you
can't find in
supermarkets.

Of tree fruits, pears are probably among the best for home planting. They are not troubled seriously by most of the common diseases or insects that attack other trees and can be grown with very little—if any—spraying. They thrive in various soils and growing conditions. Once established, pears require infrequent pruning to continue producing abundantly.

However, there have been several reasons why pears have not achieved high marks among home fruit growers. Perhaps the biggest reason has been their susceptibility to fire blight. It is a serious affliction that can cause sudden wilting and browning of new growth. Fortunately, improved varieties today are more resistant to this bacterial disease. In addition, new fungicides are available to control it.

Pears also are notoriously poor pollinators, some varieties more so than others. Some varieties require other pear varieties to achieve the necessary pollination to set fruit. For those of us with little area, pears perhaps just don't seem worth the space needed for two or three trees to provide adequate cross-pollination. A third factor is the space each standard-size tree requires.

Today interest in pears is reviving, now that fire blight can be controlled both by selecting resistant varieties that are not as susceptible to the disease and by special spray programs that can lick it.

Moreover, pear trees have been successfully reduced in size so they are more suitable for multipurpose landscaping. According to nurseries surveyed recently, demand for dwarf pears is increasing steadily. Pear trees are dwarfed by growing them grafted to a quince root. That's fortunate. Quince is one of the hardiest rootstocks among fruit trees.

In early efforts to dwarf pears, researchers found that certain varieties were not compatible with the quince root. The grafts they attempted didn't grow. Searching for ways to overcome this problem, plant breeders discovered that a compatible interstem of **Old**

Home can be used to produce a strong dwarf pear tree. Today, many excellent varieties are being made available.

Pears also have another advantage that is gaining them new friends: they respond well to espalier culture. You can train dwarf pears to trellises, create fan-shaped trees, and use them in other distinctive ways.

Earliest records of pears in the United States are traced to Salem, Massachusetts, in the early 1600s. Although fire blight did limit commercial production to Far Western states where summer rains are fewer, the renewed interest for home growing is encouraging.

Pear-tree longevity is amazing. Pears may live and produce abundantly for 100 years or more. **Kieffer** and **Tyson** are two varieties noted for their endurance and continued bearing ability.

Unlike apples, which have variations in flavor and texture but are similar and identified readily as apples even when the tasters are blindfolded, pears differ markedly in flavor. They also have a greater diversity in size, shape, and texture. You can select the small **Seckel** pears or other so-called winter types that keep well and are tasty for preserving or pickling, or the plump **Bartletts** which dribble juice with every bite.

All of the important pear varieties that are available in the United States trace their ancestry to European species, but **Kieffer** and **Barger** result from crossing European strains with a Japanese pear.

Like apples, there are some 2,000-plus varieties of pears, but only a handful are suitable for home gardens. No matter. Those that are available are superb and well worth consideration in your fruitful landscape planning.

Pomologists like to say that most pear varieties are self-unfruitful. Translated, that means you need two trees of different varieties to ensure cross-fertilization so they set and bear fruit.

Plant two or three or four of the dwarf types and you can enjoy the varied tastes and textures from these different kinds. More people today see this need for more than one pear tree as a bonus, rather than a drawback.

Here are some of the better varieties as you go shopping. Consider whether you prefer upright or spreading growth patterns as you design pears into your plantscape.

The best bet is to stick with those that are known to be resistant to fire blight if you live in the eastern United States, where summer rains and warm weather encourage this bacterial disease. **Moonglow**, **Magness**, and **Seckel** are resistant varieties that all do well in home gardens.

Moonglow bears early. The trees are vigorous and very upright in growth with large, moderately juicy fruit that is nearly free of grit cells. The fruit is mild-flavored and of good quality for dessert or cooking uses.

Magness bears late on vigorous, spreading trees. The fruit is medium-size, oval and, being tough-skinned, somewhat resistant to insect puncture or decay. The flesh is soft, very juicy, and sweet. This pear is aromatic, too. However, its pollen is completely sterile, so you'll need another pear variety to achieve cross-pollination.

Seckel pears mature late in the season. The trees are large, vigorous, and upright. Their tips are dense and their spread is small. They are amazingly productive, yielding small, symmetrical, smooth fruit. The flesh is white with a slight yellow tinge. It has been described as buttery, very juicy, aromatic, spicy. Seckel pears are known for their excellent quality for dessert or cooking.

Bartlett is superior to all varieties both for fresh use and canning. It is large, golden yellow, and highly flavored with lots of juice. The trees grow well and bear early and abundantly. Bartlett is a midseason variety, moderately susceptible to fire blight.

Gorham is another good selection. It is a Bartlett-type pear that matures early and keeps in cold storage longer than other varieties. The fruit is bright yellow with a small amount of russet around the stem end. It is hardy and less susceptible to fire blight than Bartlett.

Bosc is a different type of pear. It ripens late, but its quality is excellent, especially if it is ripened off the tree. Boscs are large pears with a dark yellow undercolor and a veil of fine russet. The flesh is white, tender, and very juicy with a tantalizing aroma. The trees develop a somewhat straggly framework of branches and are slow to begin bearing. Once it starts, this variety is very productive. It is a good pollinator.

Clapps Favorite is the best early-ripening pear. It looks similar to Bartlett but with pale lemon-yellow fruit and a bright pink cheek. Its finely textured flesh is buttery and juicy with a distinctive, delicate flavor. Its fruit is best when picked "hard ripe" and allowed to ripen fully off the tree. Unfortunately, this tasty variety is susceptible to fire blight.

Devoe is a midseason variety that grows on vigorous, productive trees. It has upright growing tendencies with large, long, golden-yellow fruit. The flesh is firm, juicy, and sweet. It is resistant to the blight and needs little maintenance once well rooted.

Among the better, newer introductions, try **Starking Delicious**, **Stark Honeysweet**, **Moonglow**, **Comice**, **Stark Ultrared Bartlett**, **Early Bearing Moonglow**, and **Max-Red Bartlett**.

For something different and now readily available in the United States from key nurseries, consider **Dwarfed Hybrid Red Anjou**, **Colette**, and **Beurre Bosc**.

Oriental pears are making a big hit. Gourmet stores sell them for rather high prices, but now you can grow and enjoy them in your home orchard, year after year.

You can try **Shinseiki**, a dwarfed Asian pear rated true gourmet in quality. Its sweet, mild juice is abundant with each bite. Shinseiki is good for salads and eating fresh. It keeps well for months when refrigerated.

Chojuro is a dwarfed hybrid, easy to grow for small backyard or even patio culture. Only head-high and 6 feet across, it has true compact growth. The fruit looks like apples but will amaze you with delicious pear flavor.

A **Hosui Asian** pear is slightly higher in acid content with a snappy, tangy taste. It is blight-resistant, self-pollinating, and provides maximum harvests, ripening in early September in horticultural zone 6. Fruit tree nurseries indicate in their catalogs which varieties are suitable for which horticultural zones. A USDA horticultural zone map is included in this book for your guidance.

The **20th Century Asian** pear produces abundant crops of pure white flesh pears ideal for snacking and salads.

Pears enjoy the same growing conditions as apples do. They prefer some cold weather to induce their needed dormant period. If they don't get sufficient winter chilling, such as in southern areas, there may be an uneven opening of flowers in spring. That unevenness may create a problem in timing sprays for codling-moth control and interfere with cross-pollination on varieties that require help from other nearby varieties.

On the other hand, most pear varieties will endure winter temperatures well below −20 degrees F. without serious injury. **Clapps Favorite**, **Seckel**, and **Anjou** types are most resistant to cold. **Bartlett** has proved somewhat less so. Pears can withstand higher summer temperatures than apples. In fact, **Bartlett** prefers higher temperatures to reach its peak quality. It is more suitable than others for southern areas.

Pears prosper even through droughts and can produce better on a wider variety of soils, including sandier or heavily wet soils, than almost any other tree fruit. For practical purposes and to avoid stressing your pear trees, plant them on soil that is deep, fertile, and well drained.

planting tips

Pears and apples not only enjoy the same growing conditions in general, but also should receive the same initial care in planting. Rather than repeat the steps here, I suggest that you consult the planting methods outlined for apples. Because pears can live for human generations, it pays to plant them well so their roots reach down and out to get the strongest possible growing start.

Pears do well in western areas of the United States. However, they won't perform satisfactorily on alkali soil or soils that are subject to excess salinity from irrigation water.

Pears can fit nicely in a group at the center of a yard or in a row along a property line. Grouping pears together produces a balanced planting effort. It also provides the closeness needed to ensure proper pollination when one of the group needs that aid from another.

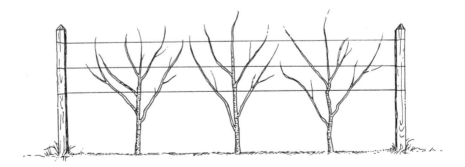

Grouping several pears along a wire trellis produces a nicely balanced effect and places trees close enough for pollination.

For hedgerow planting, space standard pear trees 8 feet apart in rows 12 feet apart. Varieties that spread may require up to 14 feet from each other and rows 24 feet apart if you are setting a mini-orchard. With dwarf-rootstock pears, you can space them as close as dwarf apples. For training to espalier distinction, read Chapter 11 on espalier growing for space sculpturing.

In Europe, a "spindlebush" system combines plantings of pears and apples. It makes sense because they enjoy the same basic growing conditions. Europeans space dwarfed pears on quince rootstock 4 to 8 feet apart, and keep trees neatly trimmed. These farmers achieve exceptional yields.

Recently in the United States, **Angers** and **Provence** quince stock has been used to produce dwarf pear trees that are more compact, denser, and more productive. We planted several during 1976, the bicentennial year, among the thirteen new dwarf fruit trees on our property. They have taken root and are thriving better than expected, considering that temperatures in Maine get mighty cold in winter.

pruning pointers

Young pear trees need some training. They should be pruned to the modified-leader system as you would prune young apple trees. In areas where fire blight is not a serious problem, trim second-year pear trees to three or four main scaffold (side) branches. In the East, where fire blight still exists despite the resistance of improved varieties, leave more scaffold branches extending from the trunk—six to eight at first. If you must prune some infected branches later, you still have a reserve that will fill out to form your mature tree.

Most pear varieties grow upright. That is a distinguishing characteristic. They may seem to be sprouting too tall. Resist the urge to tip them off, which is called "heading back." If top pruning is necessary, trim only the tallest leaders.

But go easy. Too much heading back by cutting the first tall growing tips can encourage overproduction of more soft terminal shoots. To achieve a more attractively spread appearance, try braces of wood in the crotch. This technique helps limbs spread gracefully. Remove the braces or wedges in the fall to avoid ice breakage during winter. Once pear trees begin to bear, branches will be naturally weighted into a more spreading appearance.

When trees begin maturing, there is little you need to do except remove damaged branches and prune shoots that cross or tangle every few years. That's all you need to do to keep pear trees in the desired, open shape, whether on a specimen plant, in a hedgerow, or in a specially shaped growing pattern.

Here are proper pruning steps for apple or pear tree at (from left to right) its second, third, fourth, and fifth or sixth year.

Pear fruit buds are similar to those of apples. They will have five to seven flowers at the terminal of the cluster. Pears are produced mainly from blooms on spurs, rising from the branches. They may continue yielding for six to ten years. On older trees, it is best to thin out new shoots. From time to time you can remove older branches. Younger shoots will fill in to become bearing (fruiting) wood in future years. Pear trees of bearing age should add 15 to 30 inches of growth per year.

Overpruning is unwise. Just a few cuts here and there to keep trees open to air and sun and sprays when pesticides are needed will be sufficient.

Do remove suckers from trunks, and water sprouts, those ungainly tallest shoots on branches. Fire blight disease prefers to attack young succulent growth, especially water shoots and sucker growth.

If fire blight does strike unexpectedly, take steps immediately. The bacteria overwinters in cankers under bark on limbs and large branches. These areas look darker than surrounding healthy bark. They're usually slightly sunken and rough. During warm, moist spring and summer weather, a brownish sticky liquid oozes from them. Wind, rain, and insects will carry the bacteria to succulent growth on nearby trees.

The first step is to locate these cankers and cut them out. Use a sharp knife and remove all the canker to clean wood. Then disinfect the wound with a solution of one part household bleach to nine parts water. Make sure that you disinfect your knife and pruning tools with the same solution between cuts. Cover wounds with tree-wound paint, available at garden and farm-supply stores, hardware stores, and even many chain stores these days.

Prune any brown, dead portions of each twig at least 8 inches below the infection. Remove all pruned material from the area and burn it.

. . . .

According to specialists, a streptomycin spray helps reduce fire blight spread. This spray should be used during bloom, at petal fall, and at ten-day intervals if the problem is severe in your area. However, consult your local pesticide supplier for his or her formulas and timetable depending on conditions in your locale.

fire-blight spray schedule

For areas that are threatened with fire blight, here's a suggested spray schedule. It was provided by the University of Missouri but also applies for other areas. Check the latest recommendations based on recent updated research in your area.

First Spray	When blossom clusters show tinge of pink	100 ppm* streptomycin
Second Spray	7 days after first spray	100 ppm streptomycin
Third Spray	7 days after last spray	100 ppm streptomycin
Fourth Spray	7 days after last spray	100 ppm streptomycin

*Parts per million. Streptomycin is sold under the various trade names of Agrimycin, Agristrep, and Phytomycin by various manufacturers.

fertilizing

Pears respond to the same balanced fertilizer programs you would apply to apple trees, adjusted for dwarf to standard-size trees. However, it is best to go lighter in fertilizing pears than with apples. Instead of 1 to 2 pounds around a newly established tree, reduce that amount almost to half. If suckers or water shoots grow, remove them. There's no sense letting fire blight from other areas find succulent new territory on your home grounds.

Apples, peaches, and plums usually require some hand-thinning to avoid overbearing that results in too many smaller, less flavorful fruits. Pears need relatively little thinning. Bartlett and Bosc varieties may set heavier crops from time to time. If they do have four to five fruits per cluster after petal fall, you can simply reduce that number to two to three. Remember that excessive fruit set can weigh down and snap branches.

Pears, like any other fruit trees, attract pests. Rather than duplicate spray schedules, crop by crop, I have outlined basic pest-prevention guidelines in Chapter 12.

Local conditions, whether in fire-blight areas or elsewhere, determine the precise materials and timings of pear pesticide-protection applications. County agricultural agents and state extension services publish yearly recommendations based on problems prevalent the year before and new materials that have been introduced.

These pest-control plans are free. Just call or write your county agent for details about your specific area.

harvesting

Most other fruits achieve their peaks, their most luscious, juiciest, most mouth-watering flavor, when they ripen on the tree or bush. Pears are different. They reach their highest quality when harvested in a slightly underripe stage. If they begin to fall, you may have missed the prime time for picking.

Watch your trees carefully as fruits become plump and richly colored for their variety. Then pick them when they seem full-size for the variety. The best gauge is change of color and firmness. These changes indicate increases in sugar content as your pears approach full ripeness.

The ease with which you can separate the stem from the spur is another reliable indication of time to harvest pears. Knowing exactly when to harvest is a trick you'll learn in time. It may not be the same date from year to year because growing conditions do vary.

In our pear growing over the years, I have this simple rule. When no pears have fallen but they look ripe, I pick two. One goes into the refrigerator. The other I taste. After a week, I repeat the test and also sample the first one I put in the refrigerator. Usually I can estimate when pear-picking time arrives. Then I harvest the crop for storage and ripening indoors. You can leave some on the trees if you wish but pears ripen best when removed from the trees a week or so before they would be fully ripe and placed in a paper bag or on the kitchen counter until they're ready to eat.

7

peaches, nectarines, and apricots

•

Peaches are not native

to America, but they've

won wide acclaim since

they were introduced

by early Spanish

explorers. They are

grown commercially in

thirty states and in

home gardens in nearly

all states. Next to apples, peaches are one of our most popular tree fruits.

Peach trees are naturally small; they require little space for glorious displays. Today, dwarf varieties let you enjoy tasty peaches even on balconies or in patio planters. Delicious **Bonanza** dwarf peach trees even grow indoors in pots.

Homegrown peaches offer more delicious eating pleasure than most store-bought ones. The reason is simple. Peaches are especially delicate. They bruise easily, just as ripe tomatoes do. Commercially grown varieties may be fine if allowed to ripen on the tree, but they are picked before becoming fully ripe. Also, to withstand the handling, packing, and jarring of shipment over long distances, commercial varieties of peaches have been bred to be tougher skinned.

You can grow peaches right in your own backyard or on your apartment balcony. Peaches are friendly. They're not difficult to grow either. The varieties you can select offer honest-to-goodness tree-ripe flavor you can't find anywhere else.

The fame of Georgia peaches has spread to all parts of the country. For this reason many people believe that peaches can be grown successfully only in southern areas. But orchardists in Canada grow delicious peaches. And peaches thrive in upper New York State, in Oregon, and even in some sheltered valleys along the rocky coast of Maine. It used to be difficult to grow many varieties in northern areas. However, plant breeders have developed excellent varieties that do persist and perform well in northern areas.

In fact, many of the country's best-known peaches are perfected for growing in Michigan. The climate there isn't exactly blessed with southern sunshine.

peaches

New and better varieties of peaches are being rapidly introduced. Plant breeders are responding to the increased demand for peaches by commercial growers and home gardeners as well. To provide hardier peaches, new varieties are being grafted on **Siberian** seedling rootstocks. These consistently harden off; they prepare themselves for cold weather earlier in the fall than do trees on more common stocks. This earlier hardening has resulted in much better survival rates.

For example, work at the Geneva Experiment Station in New York State revealed that trees of **Redhaven** peaches on the **Siberian C** stock carried full crops and had low bud mortality in comparison to the same Redhaven variety on other rootstocks.

The Siberian rootstock seems to have little dwarfing effect. Because of its superior climatic adaptation, fruit specialists recommend use of Siberian C rootstock or similar hardiness-transmitting types for peaches grown in northern areas.

Dwarf peach trees are listed in most nursery catalogs. They are usually budded or grafted on **Sand Cherry** roots. This means that they tend to be short-lived.Some nurseries produce dwarf peaches grafted on **Nanking Cherry** rootstocks. These are quite dwarfed and highly productive. Judging from trials in various areas of the country, they seem to be longer-lived than dwarfs created on Sand Cherry roots.

Whether you prefer the tiny dwarf peach trees that may mature to only 3 to 5 feet tall or the standard size, which grow only 8 to 15 feet high, select several different varieties of peaches to extend your harvest season. Some trees bear very early, others midseason to late in the season. Very early types include **Candor, Collins, Brighton, Harbinger**, and **Garnet Beauty**.

Early varieties include **Prairie Dawn, Reliance, Redhaven**, and **Raritan Rose**.

For midseason, choose **Triogem, Eden, Canadian Harmony, Glohaven, Vanity**, among many varieties.

You can also plant some late-ripening varieties. **Jefferson** and **Tyler** are two.

Peaches are either *Clingstone*, meaning that the pits cling to the flesh, or *Freestone*, where the pits readily separate from the flesh. For home gardens, both are useful. This feature will have no impact unless you run a cannery or wish to can most of your crop.

Candor ripens early (June to July depending on your area) with attractive oval red peaches. The flesh is medium-firm, semi-cling, juicy, and sweet. These peaches do not turn brown and are well-liked for this quality. Trees are vigorous and productive and seem medium-hardy.

Collins ripens about the same time, quite early. The medium-size peaches mature six or more weeks ahead of **Elberta**, one of the best-known commercial varieties. Collins is early, bright red with yellow flesh. It is semi-clingstone. Trees are hardy, vigorous, and productive.

Brighton is a high-quality, yellow-fleshed peach with roundish, uniformly medium-size fruit. It also is bright red on a yellow background. The flesh is medium-firm and semi-cling, juicy, and sweet. Trees are vigorous and productive.

Reliance is one of the most winter-hardy varieties. The fruit is medium-size, yellow-fleshed, and of good quality. It keeps well and is dandy for eating or preserving. Trees are highly productive and hardy in colder areas.

Red Haven is a superior variety with good winter hardiness too. The flesh is firm, finely textured, and of very good quality. It is versatile for eating, freezing, and canning, and is prolific. You should thin Red Haven or it overbears.

Canadian Harmony is large, highly colored, yellow-fleshed, firm, juicy, and nondarkening. Trees are vigorous, productive, and quite hardy.

Among late varieties preferred by many home gardeners, **Jefferson** is a large, yellow-fleshed freestone peach. It has red and orange-yellow skin with a firm, flavorful texture. Trees are vigorous and produce heavy fruit set, which requires thinning.

Tyler ripens late on vigorous trees. The fruits are firm, flavorful, and freestone. This variety, too, may require hand-thinning because it tends to bear heavily.

For really cold climates, nurseries offer **Reliance**, which can withstand temperatures that fall to −25 degrees F., yet yields full crops of delicious peaches.

If leaf curl disease is a problem, try **Curlfree Peach**. It is winter-hardy, and also resists leaf-curl disease. It is almost identical to **Red Haven**, but has a bold flavor and ripens almost one week earlier.

Other improved peach varieties are **Stark Early White** giant peach, **Stark Elberta Queen** peach, and **Burbank July Elberta** peach.

Other disease-resistant newer varieties include **Com-Pact Redhaven** peach, **Stark Compact Elberta** peach, and **Belle of Georgia** peach. Some, such as **Stark Encore** and **Earliglo**, are special cultivars—special hybrids—and qualify for plant patents. These are somewhat more expensive, but their extra values from hardiness to disease resistance are worth the initial cost.

nectarines

If you don't like fuzz on your peaches, try nectarines.

Nectarines are somewhat more susceptible to brown rot than peaches are. However, this problem is controlled quite easily with an effective combination pesticide and fungicide application program.

Smooth skin and delicious flavor make nectarines an increasingly popular fresh fruit for home landscapes. Their culture is identical to that of peaches. Most nectarines have the advantage of being self-fruitful. In other words, they pollinate themselves readily. Nursery catalogs advise you which varieties need other varieties for proper pollination. There are many more nectarines than space permits me to list here, but the following ones are good.

Lexington is a productive, medium-size, yellow-fleshed variety. The flavor is sweet. Trees are hardy and resistant to spring frosts.

Cherokee is a fine yellow-fleshed nectarine. The fruit is large and bright-colored with firm, juicy flesh and semi-cling habit. Trees are productive and medium-hardy, making this variety better for southern areas.

Tiger is a Stark exclusive. It is exceptionally winter-hardy, resistant to brown rot, and a fine freestone variety of good quality. Trees are productive, and may need some hand-thinning.

Redgold is a very high-quality, beautifully colored, and firm-fleshed variety. It is winter and spring bud-hardy too.

Pocahontas is a very early, yellow-fleshed semi-cling nectarine. The flesh is juicy and sweet. Trees are productive and medium-hardy in northern areas.

Stark Crimson Gold nectarine is a Zaifger cultivar that is winter-hardy, ripens early and yields large crops of bright red fruit.

Mericrest is a University of New Hampshire development, a tangy, delicious nectarine that shrugs off snow and ice and is hardy to 125 degrees F. It ripens in August.

apricots

Apricots prefer well-drained, light- to medium-textured soils of reasonable fertility. They bloom early, so a site with good air drainage is important to avoid spring frost damage. Most apricots are self-fruitful, but it is wise to plant two varieties to ensure maximum fruit set. Because apricots suffer in harsh, cold areas, they are best grown in parts of the country that have moderate temperatures. They can be grown in northerly climates, but extra efforts should be taken to protect apricots from winter winds.

As with peaches and nectarines, many varieties are available. Catalogs will advise you which are best for what areas. Some are more hardy than others.

Alfred is a productive, good-quality apricot that thrives in the climates of the northeast. The fruit ripens late in July and is medium-size and bright orange with a sweet, rich flavor to its firm, juicy flesh.

Goldcot is a winner according to Michigan Experiment Station researchers after thousands of field tests. The fruit is nearly round, the flesh medium orange with a fine texture. Trees are exceptionally strong, above average in winter hardiness, and self-fruitful. Heavy fruit set may require hand-thinning.

Sungold is unusually hardy in cold climates, too. It produces heavily with freestone fruit that ripens in mid to late season.

Moongold bears earlier but is not as tasty as Sungold. Moongold produces heavy crops with a sweet taste and is good for fresh use and jam or all purpose.

Stella is a hardy Russian-type apricot that is very cold-resistant. The fruit is medium-size, golden in color, freestone, and delicious. It thrives where peaches can be grown.

As you shop for peach, nectarine, and apricot trees, keep in mind that they are less tolerant of severe conditions than apples or pears and susceptible to sharp variations in weather. Apricots especially may be a gamble even in sites just right for peaches. The apricot blooms so early that it can suffer badly from late spring frosts.

planting tips

Peach trees and their fruit buds are perhaps the most tender of all fruit trees that can be grown in northern areas. So your site selection is important in order to give them every chance they can get to please you and satisfy your craving for juicy ripe crops each year.

Peaches love the sun. Severe winter temperatures, below −15 degrees F., will destroy most fruit buds. So will late frosts, if buds have progressed to certain growth stages when the cold snap occurs. This can happen after several weeks of mild weather that encourages buds to swell.

When looking for the perfect spot for your peach trees, consider several factors. (These points hold true for apricots and nectarines, too.) Avoid frost pockets, those low-lying spots where cold air accumulates. They are death to peaches and their relatives. Good air and soil drainage will help to maintain the highest temperatures during frosty spring nights and even during wintery cold periods. Usually peach trees should be planted in an area higher than adjacent land. However, if that means exposing peach trees to prevailing winds that dry and freeze the plants, pick another site.

For northern areas, and even in more southerly areas of the mid-Atlantic states, you should select cold-hardy varieties. Unusually cold weather in Georgia, Florida, and California has been known to destroy large portions of peach crops.

The best bet for peaches is a protected, sheltered area of your grounds. It should be warmed by sun by day and shielded from extremes of winds or frosty air settling at night. You can build a wind-screen of burlap on posts to protect young trees from chilling winds. Or use a 5- to 6-foot-tall board fence.

If peaches have a chance to establish strong rootholds on fertile, well-drained soil, they can build up resistance to the cold. A deep sandy loam soil with gravelly clay subsoil is ideal. If your land

A simple burlap or canvas screen protects young trees from winter winds.

doesn't have it, you can improve the planting area for each individual tree. Later you can work on improving the surrounding areas.

Dig up the soil. Discard any that is really poor, rocky, or filled with debris or wet clay lumps. Then prepare an improved soil mix: combine 2 parts good topsoil with 1 part sand and 1 part leaf mold, composted humus, or peat moss. Composted humus is best. Mix it thoroughly.

Next, place a layer of gravel, about 2 inches deep, in the bottom of the hole, below the depth the tree roots will reach initially.

Put well-rotted manure and topsoil, mixed together, on the gravel bed, about 3 to 4 inches deep. Next add a layer of the improved soil mix you have prepared. Then begin the planting process. Spread the roots naturally without bending or crowding. Add the improved soil mixture. Tamp it down. Water well to settle the soil. Add more of the improved topsoil. Tamp that down too. Leave a saucer-shaped depression around the tree or shrub. It will collect rain and will direct water from your sprinkler or hose to the root area of your newly planted tree or shrub. The illustration shows how to prepare the site, improve the soil, and plant any tree or shrub well.

Peaches prefer spring planting, as soon as soil can be prepared. It pays, of course, to get the site you have selected ready the previous fall. Giving them the advantage of a spring start and a fall season's growth to set their roots well and acclimate themselves to their new home is desirable.

Peach trees enjoy the same tender loving care you would give to other fruit trees at planting time. Perhaps some extra care is warranted. If the trees you buy have bare roots, be sure to keep them moist from the moment they arrive to the time you set them in the soil by heeling in—placing roots in a trench and covering with soil until you have time to plant them—or planting them.

Soaking peach, nectarine, and apricot trees in water for several hours before planting is a good practice. You should also keep roots moist with wet burlap if you have removed them from their pail of water and delayed the actual planting for any reason.

Plant them as you would other valuable fruit trees. Detailed step-by-step directions are outlined in the planting section of Chapter 5, Apples.

Because peach trees and their cousins are tender, never use manure or fertilizer in the soil mix or added into the hole as you plant the trees. It can be lethal, so delay fertilizing these trees until several weeks after they have been planted. If the soil is reasonably fertile and you provided an improved mixture during planting, there is no need to apply fertilizer the first year. However, if you did not improve the soil, a cupful or two of 10–6–4 spread in a ring 18 inches around the trunk of newly planted trees can be scratched into the soil two or three weeks after planting.

When you plant, be certain that the graft union is 1 to 3 inches *below* the soil level. This is different from the usual procedure for other fruit trees. Peaches are more tender. If suckers arise from the ground, just prune them away. Water well twice each week if no rain falls for several weeks.

fertilizing

Once your peaches, nectarines, or apricots are well rooted, it's time to satisfy their growing needs. Nitrogen is the most important element for them; very often it is the only nutrient they need.

Too little nitrogen can result in low yields, poor fruit size, and excessive injury from cold. Too much plant food may cause overly rapid growth, poor fruit color, and excessive injury from cold. The amount of nitrogen that peach trees need is based on growth and performance of the individual tree. You should expect them to make 18 to 24 inches of new terminal growth annually. In mature, bearing trees, at least 12 inches is optimum to maintain good vigor.

Unlike other fruit trees, peaches and their relatives must be catered to individually. Get out a ruler. Check their growth. Watch bloom, fruit set, and harvest yields. Usually a bearing, mature tree needs about one pound of nitrogen per year for best results. You can apply that in a circle scratched into the soil around the tree 24 to 36 inches from the trunk. Peaches and their friends don't like to compete with sod or grass of any kind. It is best to mulch beneath peaches or clean-cultivate to keep weeds and grasses from interfering with their performance.

Once trees have begun bearing, a 10–6–4 or similar garden fertilizer, high in nitrogen, will usually keep them well satisfied.

In experiments by peach-growing experts, various fertilizing programs were tested over a period of years. Fertilizer rates per tree of bearing size to six years were 1 pound of 16 percent nitrogen or ½ pound of 3 percent nitrogen, 1 pound of 20 percent superphosphate, and ¼ pound of muriate of potash.

Nitrogen fertilizer resulted in an increased tree size. This increase was achieved whether nitrogen was used alone or in combination with phosphorus or potash or both.

Tree growth was not significantly improved by phosphorus or potash. Trees receiving high nitrogen and smaller amounts of the other ingredients produced about three times as much fruit as trees that received no plant food.

Peach trees are naturally smaller than other types of fruit trees. Dwarf varieties may be grown successfully in large tubs.

If you try potting peaches on your patio, give special attention to planting them. A gravel layer in whatever container you use is necessary. Then add the improved soil mixture mentioned earlier. Dwarf peach trees in restricted growing situations need extra attention to their habitat. Go easy on the amount of fertilizer you apply to dwarf peach trees, especially in containers. Read and follow directions on the fertilizer container.

pruning pointers

Peaches, nectarines, and apricots prefer open growth to achieve the fullest, ripest perfection from proper sun and air circulation.

Dwarf peaches need little care except occasional clipping here and there to maintain their lovely diminutive shape and form.

Training standard peach, nectarine, and apricot trees requires special care when they are young. A tree that is trained correctly will usually live years longer than one left to choke itself by over-branching. The trained tree will resist winter injury to the trunk and main scaffold branches and be able to carry heavier fruit loads with less limb breakage.

Here's a step-by-step guide from the ground up after planting.

One-year-old peach trees will arrive from mail-order nurseries usually as a branched whip. Often side branches are weak and too small for framework branches. Cut them back to spurs leaving three or four buds on each. The tree itself should be cut back to about 36 inches above the ground.

After the first season, remove all side branches that form a narrow angle of less than 45 degrees with the trunk. Remove any branches that are only a few inches above the ground. They will be too low to produce any fruit and will just hinder regular care.

Also, if any two limbs of approximately equal size divide the tree into a Y shape, cut off one. Remove suckers or even strong branches that fill in and shade the center.

To keep your peach, apricot, and nectarine trees well balanced, cut back stronger framework branches slightly. After the second season, continue pruning to develop an open-centered, spreading tree. Remove any limbs that tend to grow up through or across the center. Eliminate any center leaders and continue to cut away suckers growing straight up. However, leave the rest of the one-year growth throughout the tree.

After two or three years, a well-grown tree will have a trunk 4 to 6 inches in circumference and a good supply of fruit buds on branches. Pruning now requires extra care. Moderate pruning will result in production of as much as a bushel of peaches the third summer. Severe pruning will reduce or may eliminate the third summer's crop.

After the third year, peach trees should produce substantial crops annually. They may live twenty to thirty-five years, depending on the care they receive. Continue to prune to maintain that open center.

Peaches are produced on wood that grew the previous season. That's why continued pruning is necessary to stimulate new wood growth, which will bear well for you the next year. Depending on your landscape use, you can train peaches moderately. However, if they are primarily as specimens or part of a home mini-orchard, try to keep them about 12 feet high. That size is hardier and easier to maintain, prune, and harvest.

After several years' growth, peach trees can develop two or three scaffold branches of great strength. Two are better for overall balance. Keep pruning to a minimum after the first few years, just enough to maintain shape, remove dead or damaged branches, and stimulate next year's fruiting wood.

Thinning nearly every year may be necessary to ensure a crop of plump, full-sized peaches. Otherwise trees may overbear, break branches, and set too many fruits that won't be as large and tasty. Hand-thinning is easy.

Consider that it takes 380 peaches, 2 inches in diameter, to fill a bushel, but only 190 of 2–½-inch peaches to fill the same bushel. Wouldn't you rather have those bigger, tastier ones?

Thin peaches so they are spaced 2 to 3 inches apart on the tree. Proper thinning will also increase winter hardiness, according to experiment-station reports at agricultural colleges.

pest control

Brown rot and powdery mildew may trouble your peach trees and their relatives. Fortunately, modern fungicides can prevent these problems. Insects, too, can attack at times. Details on pest control, based on a sound pest-prevention plan, are included in Chapter 12, which covers spray schedules for all fruits.

. . . .

harvesting

"Mature" and "ripe" are often used interchangeably by farmers and orchardists. Actually, these words describe distinct and separate processes. Maturity involves fullness of growth and indicates completeness of development of the peaches, nectarines, and apricots, and other fruits as well.

Ripeness takes place after the fruit is mature. It involves the softening of the flesh and the development of juiciness and flavor. This stage may occur before or after fruit is taken from the tree; peaches also ripen after picking. The best way to tell when your peaches are near their peak maturity is to watch the ground color: the undercolor of the skin. It may be greenish or greenish yellow at first.

As ripeness approaches, the ground color will become more yellowish or orange overall. The red color may brighten, but is never as good an indicator of ripeness as the ground color. Feel, of course, is helpful, but pinching peaches does bruise them. Remember that not all peaches mature at the same time. Selective picking is in order—perhaps three or more times. Take only the largest, most mature, and fully colored ones each time.

If you plant several peach trees and have done your homework on early- to late-season varieties, you can enjoy the best flavor that peaches have to offer from early summer right through the fall.

The planting, pruning, thinning, and harvesting methods for nectarines and apricots are similar to those for peaches. However, apricots bloom earlier. These delicious fruits are especially tender, so be certain to insist on the hardiest types. Winters in northern areas can thwart even your best efforts to grow them.

Look around your land. Pick that fertile, well-drained area. Improve the soil and start planting. Peach-harvesting time in your backyard is just a few years away.

8

plums

•

Plums offer a greater

selection of species and

varieties adapted to the

different climate and

soil conditions that are

found across America

than any other fruit

tree. Some can tolerate

extreme cold; others

prefer and thrive in

more temperate climates; still others grow well in warmer regions. Being relatively small in size, plum trees can fit into a variety of garden designs. They bloom beautifully in spring and provide foliage displays in summer and fruit to savor all year round. As you scan your grounds this year, pick a spot or two for plum trees.

Plums, too, can be trained in distinctive patterns, as indicated in Chapter 11 on espaliers. Even without much extra attention, plums provide cascades of bloom and bountiful harvests of succulent fruit from relatively small space.

More than 2,000 varieties of plums have been grown in the United States, according to best estimates by plant scientists. Today your choice is wide and flavorful. The most important type is descended from European plums. It is moderately vigorous stock with thick leaves that have glossy green sheen above and paler green color below. Fruit grows on spurs and varies in size, color, and shape, with distinctive differences in flesh color and flavor, too.

The plum family from European ancestors has five basic groups. One is the **prune** group, which can be picked and dried with its pit intact.

The **Greengage** group is more easily identified by its round fruit with green, yellow, or reddish flesh, and sweet and juicy flavor.

The **Yellow Egg** group is primarily a commercial canning type.

The **Imperatrice** group includes most of the blue plums. These trees typically bear heavily, producing medium-size, oval-shaped fruit with firm flesh. They are not as flavorful as other varieties.

The **Lombard** group is similar to the Imperatrice type but is red, usually smaller, and somewhat lower in quality.

American plums are another family, native to the United States and Canada. They include species suitable for fresh use or cooking. Plant breeders have found them useful as rootstock on which more desired varieties can be grafted to achieve a hardiness for colder areas.

. . . .

Japanese plums are typically early bloomers. For this reason they may be susceptible to frost. Many are as winter hardy as peaches and can be grown under the same range of conditions. Others won't survive far-northern climates. The Japanese plums are distinguished by their larger size and tendency to be heart-shaped. They may be red, yellow, or a blend between. The trees tend to be more colorful at blooming time because they have a more abundant flowering habit.

Plums may be self-pollinating or require cross-pollination from a nearby similar plum variety. Nurseries can advise you. There's not much sense in planting just one that you think will bear, waiting several years, and then realizing that another tree is needed for cross-pollination.

As you look around your land, estimate spacing for plums as you would for peaches. At maturity they will take the same space as standard peach trees. You can, with proper pruning, keep them in bounds. However, since they are reasonably small, it's best to give them the room they need for their most abundant performance.

Here is a brief list of some of the better plums you can select. Mail-order nurseries offer others that may be more suited to specific growing conditions in certain areas. If you have doubts, it pays to ask. When you put the work into planting, tending, and cultivating them, you have every right to know that they will prosper in your area.

european plums

The European plums comprise the most important and widest selection of types and some plums of the best quality available. Many require cross-pollination. Even varieties classed as self-fruitful may produce much better and more abundant crops when cross-pollination from other trees is provided.

DeMontfort is an old French blue plum. It bears in August, is medium-size and roundish oval, and has dark purple fruit that is juicy, sweet, and rich. It is highly regarded as a freestone type.

French Damson is one of the largest Damson plums. It is vigorous and productive. The fruit measures 1–¼ to 1–½ inches in diameter and is delightful for making plum preserves.

Greengage has been cultivated in Europe for hundreds of years. You can grow it here quite easily. The fruit is medium-size, yellowish green, mottled with red. In Europe, it is considered the ideal dessert plum; tender, juicy, rich in melting fresh flavor. If space is limited, perhaps this should be your first choice.

For early plums, try **Leaton Gage**. It has high quality and is fairly productive. Trees are vigorous growers.

Oullins is an early-ripening Gage type, one of the most attractive and largest available. **Reine Red** is a Red Gage that ripens late.

Oneide is a late, reddish-black, prune-type plum. It has proved consistently productive and is quite self-fruitful.

Stanley is a prune-type plum. Trees are hardy and vigorous and produce large crops annually. The flesh is greenish yellow, juicy, sweet, and firm, good for eating or cooking.

Yakima is a vigorous, upright-growing variety. The fruit is very large, oblong, and a bright mahogany red. The flesh is tender, firm, sweet, and yellow; it's ideal for dessert use.

Vision is a highly vigorous and productive plum. Trees are spreading. The fruit is large and blue-skinned with yellow flesh. It is high quality and freestone.

If you live in colder climates, here are some plums that have cold-hardiness:

Mount Royal is a prune type, blue in color. It makes a great dessert, jam, or preserve. It has survived extreme cold in test growing conditions of Canada.

Purple Heart is a plum with superior winter-hardiness developed in New Hampshire. It has deep red fruits of medium size with sweet red flesh. The tree is low and spreading and fits beautifully into landscapes.

japanese plums

Japanese plums have been favored by many plum fanciers for their taste and large size. If you prefer this type, remember that nearly all Japanese plums require cross-pollination. At least two different varieties should be planted to ensure that they bear a crop.

Formosa is recommended for its large, attractive oval fruits. Trees bear biannually, yielding greenish-yellow fruit overlaid with red. The flesh is firm, juicy, and sweet.

Santa Rosa is one of Luther Burbank's (one of the world's leading plant hybridizers) more noteworthy developments. It is a prolific bearer with large, attractive fruits.

Burbank is a round plum that ripens early. Trees are hardy, both themselves and their buds. It produces heavily, yielding medium to large fruits that are juicy and sweet. These trees are low-growing and somewhat drooping, with a tendency to be distinctly flat-topped. They require cross-pollination.

Mariposa plum is large and purplish red with blood red flesh that is sweet and nicely juicy. It is very winter-hardy but also needs cross-pollination.

Shiro bears early, rewarding you with bright yellow plums with bluish bloom. The flesh is light yellow, juicy, sweet, and favored for dessert or cooking. Trees are upright and spreading, large and vigorous.

Burmosa is another early bearer, moderately productive, and vigorous with large, round to oval fruit. The flesh is sweet and mild in flavor, and of good quality for eating fresh.

planting tips

Plums don't grow true from their pits. Instead, nurseries must propagate desired varieties by budding seedlings onto hardier rootstock in the nursery, as they do for peaches. Plums are grown mainly on **Myrobalan** stocks, but some plant breeders do produce them on seedlings of peach or Japanese apricots.

The **Myrobalan** stock has advantages. It is tolerant of poor soil conditions and adapts to a wide range of soils, from sandy to clay loam. It also has proved hardy and deep-rooted and has excellent longevity.

Plums can be dwarfed. Some nurseries offer this choice, although the naturally small size of plum trees may make dwarfing unnecessary. Breeders have used the **Western Sand Cherry** as a dwarfing stock for varieties of European plums. When it's used for Japanese varieties, the resulting trees are very small—only 4 to 5 feet tall. That quality is handy if space is severely limited for the two or three needed to ensure proper pollination with Japanese types.

In some areas of the country, plum orchards and home gardens have been attacked by an underground microscopic nematode, or eelworm. Today, plum and peach stocks are available that are resistant to root-knot nematode. Soil fumigation before planting, in areas that have a history of such infestation, is advisable. Your county agricultural agent most likely knows whether that would be necessary in your locale. It's tricky to do, so if there is a problem where you live, particularly in southern areas, consider planting fruit trees other than plum or peach.

Space plums the same as peach trees. Many nurseries offer started plums, since grafting or budding time in the nursery lets several lateral branches form on the trunk. However, you also may get plums as one-year-old seedlings that have the same unbranched whiplike appearance as young apple and pear trees.

. . . .

pruning pointers

Here's a general training rule. Plums that have an upright-growing habit such as **Stanley**, **Santa Rosa**, and similar varieties should be trained to a modified leader system, much as you train young apple trees. The same holds true for many of the European types, which tend to be larger and more upright.

The Japanese-type plums—with their more spreading, lower growth—are best trained to the open system, as you would peach trees. Rather than repeat all the details for pruning apple and peach trees, I refer you to the pruning pointers in those chapters.

Japanese varieties of plums seem to do best when pruned to four to five main scaffold branches. They also tend to produce more unwanted lateral shoots and water sprouts. That just means you'll need to pay more attention to cutting back excess lateral growth and removing sucker shoots or water sprouts.

Mature plum trees bear fruit along branches of one-year-old wood as well as on vigorous spurs of older wood. You should expect shoot growth of about 12 to 24 inches on young trees. Mature trees will produce about 10 inches of new growth each year.

Japanese plums tend to overbear. You can control this tendency with somewhat heavier pruning as well as thinning of extra young fruits as they form.

Plums have another unusual habit: they tend to drop young fruit a short time after setting it. That's normal, so don't become alarmed. But do check for insect damage that may cause excessive fall of young fruit. A little fruit drop is helpful. It is the tree's natural way of thinning itself. After drop occurs, check the fruit set. If there still are too many tiny plums too close together (clusters of more than three), hand-thin them as you would for peaches.

fertilizing

Fertilizing is necessary in order to maintain the vigor and productivity of your plum trees. Since plums prosper with the same care on the same type of soil and cultivation as peaches, consult that section of Chapter 7.

Plum trees, especially the Japanese types, respond cheerfully to espalier training. You can tie them into distinctive shapes and adjust your pruning efforts to create unusual forms and fancies. See Chapter 11 on espalier design.

pest control

For details about pest control for such uglies as the plum curculio and other insects that may attack your plums, as well as disease-control recommendations, consult the general pest-control guidelines in Chapter 12.

harvesting

Some plum trees bear early, others mid to late in the season. When plums seem to be well filled out, plump, and mature, begin to check them every day or so. The time to pick them depends on the use you plan to make of your plums.

For canning, preserving, and other cooking purposes, it is best to pick plums when they are firm-ripe. They will retain their shape and perform better in cooking and canning at that stage of slight underripeness.

However, if you plan to make jams, preserves, and jellies, wait until plums are fully ripe. They will then give you higher natural sugar content for a sweeter end product.

For eating, the riper the better. Just bite into one or two a day as they approach the ripest appearance on the tree. Your taste will tell you when they're truly ready.

Color is also helpful in judging ripeness. Most varieties will change markedly within a week before they are ready. With green plums, you'll notice that the green gives way to yellowish green before adding that pinkish blush some varieties attain.

Blue and purple plums change gradually from greenish blue to increasingly darker shades until they are fully ripe. Red plums also change within ten days from their light tints to the darker color of fully mature and ripe fruit.

9

cherries

•

Most of the cultivated

cherries today are

derived from two

species. Once is the

sour cherry, from which

both the light- and

dark-colored varieties

have developed.

Another type—the

sweet cherry—holds its

own in popularity even though sour varieties make better pies. Most of the cherry varieties suitable for growing in the United States are descendants of stock from France, England, Holland, and Germany. Since cherries produce more or less true to type from seed, it is difficult to trace exact lineage. However, fruit breeders are hybridizing even better varieties worth trying today.

Cherry trees grow to medium height, 12 to 20 feet, between the size of standard apples and standard peaches. For that reason, they fit neatly into many home plantings. They also bloom earlier than most other fruits. Their more graceful shape and abundance at harvesttime have made them favorites through the years.

A complete list of these delicious tiny fruits would take pages. More than a thousand varieties have been grown at one time or another in this country.

Some types are well known, for their popularity fresh or for pie making. **Bing** and **Montmorency** are two. Others are less well known, yet even better for home growing than commercially suited varieties.

Sweet-cherry trees tend to grow larger, with upright growth patterns, much like apples. Sour-cherry trees mature in a more spreading shape and closer to the size of peach trees.

Sweet cherries have the disadvantage of being self-unfruitful. That means you should plant two compatible varieties near each other to ensure proper cross-pollination. Most varieties will successfully pollinate other varieties. However, four—**Bing, Emperor Francis, Lambert,** and **Napoleon**—will not pollinate each other. Nevertheless, you can grow them. All it takes is planting another variety to ensure an effective fruit set.

Sour cherries, unlike their sweet cousins, are self-fruitful. Even one tree will bloom, pollinate itself, and bear well.

Cherries have been known to suffer from diseases, but thanks to plant breeders and their ability to produce virus-free stock, cherries can now be started better and free from one former problem. Improved pesticides and fungicides also make it possible to keep these trees thriving, well protected from other formerly troublesome diseases.

Two other factors should be considered as you mull over cherry growing as part of your outdoor plantscape. The tart (sour) type is fairly hardy, about as much so as most apple varieties. However, buds can be lost to cold winters and/or late frosts. Don't worry if a crop is missed in some years—trees will keep growing for future harvests. Sweet-cherry trees are slightly less tolerant of cold weather than peach trees. If you are living in a cold northern region, perhaps it is best to avoid them.

Three different rootstocks are used for producing cherry trees. **Mazzard** and **Mahaleb** seedling cherries and **Stockton Morello** softwood cuttings are utilized most frequently by nurseries. Mazzard is the main stock used on the West Coast for sweet cherries and other fruit trees as well because its trees are larger and resistant to root-knot nematode, borers, and other problems.

Mazzard also is preferred for sweet and sour cherries in eastern states where winter temperatures are not too extreme. However, in the East and North, Mahaleb rootstock has proved hardier and more drought-resistant. The Morello stock is better suited for southern and western areas as a carrier for sweet cherries. It causes trees to be semidwarf in size.

Here are some leading varieties of sweet cherries:

Emperor Francis is a large, dark red cherry. It resists cracking and is tasty. This is a promising new variety worth trying.

Hedelfingen ripens fairly late. It thrives in Canada and is a large, firm-fleshed black cherry, resistant to cracking in summer heat.

Ranier trees are vigorous and productive and bear early. They are hardy with large, firm, high-quality fruit, as sweet as Bing cherries. The skin is yellow with a pink blush.

Napoleon is another hardy, high-quality yellow cherry worth trying.

Stella is the first self-fruitful sweet cherry. It has large, dark red fruit, on productive trees, but is somewhat tender in areas with severe winters.

Van also has large black fruit on large, highly productive trees.

Vogue also has large black, shiny fruit with a small pit. The flesh is firm and sweet. Trees are very productive, but are susceptible to brown rot.

Among tart or sour cherries, consider these.

Montmorency, Meteor, North Star, and **Mesabi** can all withstand fairly cold winters even as far north as New Hampshire.

Montmorency is a large tree, vigorous and upright but somewhat spreading, with drooping lower branches. The fruit is large, ranging from light to dark red. The flesh is pale yellow with a reddish tinge. It tends to be freestone.

Meteor is similar to Montmorency but has somewhat larger fruit of more oblong shape. Trees are medium-size, upright, very hardy, and productive.

Nurseries provide a wider list of cherry varieties suitable for various growing regions. Always check which varieties will be hardy enough for winter in your area.

Early Richmond is a medium-size tree, vigorous and upright, with a dense round top that tends to spread. Its fruit is large and dark red, with pale yellow flesh of good quality.

Consider the characteristics and hardiness of each tree, and select the type you wish for its purpose in your landscape. For planning purposes, any site that is suitable for peaches should prove equally satisfactory for growing cherries.

Cherries prefer well-drained soil and respond to fertilizing with nitrogen just as peaches do. But cherries, possibly more than most other fruit trees, require adequate drainage. Soggy, heavier soils that hold water will harm them.

You can improve heavy soils, but it's an uphill fight to get them right for the best cherry growing. On the other hand, sandy soils that dry out won't suffice either. These are easier to improve with the addition of organic matter, as per the guidelines in Chapter 2. But, as sensitive as cherries are to late frosts, poor soils, and extreme winters, it pays to pick just the right spot.

Tart and sweet cherries enjoy full sun. It helps them ripen to juicy perfection. Sunny locations also dry off leaves faster, thereby thwarting mildews and other problems that may occur from time to time in warm, damp weather.

planting tips

Sour cherries can be planted as close as 15 to 18 feet apart. Their spreading, graceful growth pattern will grace your lawn. Since they are self-pollinating, they can be intermingled with other fruit trees and don't need to be near other cherries.

The larger, sweet-cherry varieties have a typical upright growth and require more growing room. Allow 24 to 30 feet between them. Do plan for several in a group, since they require a neighboring sweet variety for proper pollination.

Some sweet-cherry trees tend to spread as they reach maturity. One-year-old trees usually arrive as straight whips with few—if any—lateral branches. You can buy older trees, but it is easier to prune and train these youngsters. Also, there is little difference in the time they will begin to bear between one-year-old transplants and more mature stock.

Local nurseries may offer balled and burlapped or container-grown sweet-cherry trees already through their first pruned shaping. Planted properly, they'll do well.

Plant sweet cherries as you would plant apples or pears. (See details in those chapters.) Cherries are somewhat more tender, so be careful of the buds along the trunk. They can rub off easily, thereby eliminating a chance for good laterals to form in the right spots.

sweet~cherry pruning pointers

After the tree's first year at your home, lateral branches should have begun to form. Retain four to five main ones spaced around the trunk, beginning 18 to 24 inches from the ground. Choose only those that form over 45-degree angles with the trunks. Remove those that form narrower crotches.

Retain a central leader and follow the general pruning directions you would for apple trees. The same basic steps apply each year in the training of sweet cherries. If you wish to try espalier, save that urge for the smaller, sour-cherry trees.

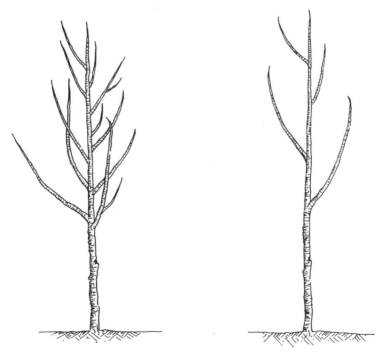

A cherry tree with too many branches, shown on the left, should be pruned as shown on the right for better shape and bearing potential in the future.

During the first few years, continue to select appropriate side branches until your tree has at least five well-distributed limbs. You may wish to do some thinning out to eliminate shoots that tend to grow up, cross, or turn to the center. Cut branches to form outward-growing limbs to achieve a more graceful and spreading appearance. As cherries begin to bear, they will require little pruning. Just remove damaged or diseased branches as you find them, with clean cuts to prevent insects or diseases from entering limbs or trunk. Keep an eye on the tree's overall shape and remove any suckers.

Sweet cherries form much less lateral growth than do sour cherries. That makes pruning easier. However, they tend to get tall. If you wish to keep them in bounds, head the leader and tallest branches back to about 15 to 18 feet, so they remain within a manageable 20-foot height.

If long limbs produce a whorl of side limbs at long intervals, reduce these to two or three the first dormant season after they have formed. Postponing this job for a few seasons and pruning these whorls later may cause some stunting of the tree.

sour-cherry pruning pointers

Sour cherries naturally tend toward spreading growth. They should be pruned as you would a peach tree.

Remove weak, smaller side branches back to one bud. Keep the lowest branch no lower than 12 to 18 inches from the ground. Allow three or four side branches to grow around the main trunk. These will produce the basic scaffold for your mature tree.

Sour-cherry trees grow more slowly than peach trees do, so less pruning is needed after the first few years of training. Prune sour-cherry trees lightly during these first five to seven years just to correct growth pattern and promote the tree's symmetry. Sour cherries may produce denser foliage and an overabundance of

◀ Stark (RL) Colonnade (TM) apple tree, an innovative and welcome new approach to fruitful home planting designed for container-growing culture. *Photo courtesy Stark Bros. Nurseries and Orchards.*

▶

Starking Hardy Giant Asian pear. *Photo courtesy Stark Bros. Nurseries and Orchards.*

◀

Starkrimson Red Delicious apples. *Photo courtesy Stark Bros. Nurseries and Orchards.*

◄
Red Bartlett
Stark pear.
*Photo courtesy
Stark Bros.
Nurseries and
Orchards.*

►
Glohaven peach.
*Photo courtesy Stark
Bros. Nurseries
and Orchards.*

◄
Stark SunGlo nectarine.
*Photo courtesy Stark Bros.
Nurseries and Orchards.*

◄

Sweetheart Stark
apricot.
*Photo courtesy Stark
Bros. Nurseries and
Orchards.*

►

Delicious Burbank plums are
highly productive.
Photo courtesy Burpee Seed Co.

◄

Shiro plum.
*Photo courtesy Stark
Bros. Nurseries and
Orchards.*

▶
A profusion of
Montmorency
cherries.
*Photo courtesy
Burpee Seed Co.*

◀
Bing cherries.
*Photo courtesy Stark Bros.
Nurseries and Orchards.*

▶
A harvest of
home-grown
chestnuts.
*Photo courtesy
Chestnut Hill
Nursery.*

twigs. If that happens, do some thinning in order to give the tree sun and air.

As trees mature, extra attention is necessary to keep them in bounds. Reduce tall upright branches to form outward-growing ones. In all pruning of sour cherries, keep in mind the basic methods for peach-tree training. Reread the peach chapter as a guide. Your objective is to keep the top of trees open to allow lots of light to enter and provide good air circulation.

As a general rule of green thumb, young nonbearing sweet cherries should produce an annual shoot growth of 22 to 36 inches. Nonbearing sour-cherry trees will make annual growth of 12 to 24 inches. As these trees mature to bearing years, they should be producing 8 to 10 inches of new shoot length per year.

fertilizing

Tests by commercial growers and college researchers, and reports from home gardeners all confirm the same fact: cherries, whether sweet or sour, respond to the same fertilizing program that promotes best growth and productivity in peaches. Rather than repeat that information here, I refer you to the nourishing of peach trees and recommend these directions. Sweet cherries need somewhat less nitrogen than sour varieties.

pest control

Cherries can be harmed by fungus diseases and by insects. Your first line of defense should be insect control because insects can carry disease organisms from infected trees in the area to your trees.

Brown rot and leaf spot are most common. Mildews may occur during warm, wet weather. Modern fungicides used in a preventive

spraying plan can provide protective barriers against these problems.

Cherry aphids, plum curculio, and fruit flies are the most common insect pests of cherries. These too can be easily prevented
with a careful pest-control plan. For additional information see
Chapter 12.

In some areas, other specific problems may occur. It pays to
contact local authorities from county agents to garden-center or
nursery specialists. They know local conditions best and can guide
you in your efforts to keep your cherries thriving.

Deer can eat buds and strip bark from trees. Your best bet is
fencing them out or getting help from your local game warden.

Birds have an uncanny knack of sensing just when cherries begin to ripen. For some reason they tend to prefer sour cherries to
sweet ones. Netting to prevent this threat by birds is necessary. It
is available in dark green or black mesh and will blend in with the
foliage to thwart those winged predators.

Cherry leaf spot can be a problem, so it pays to attend to fallen,
infected leaves. Rake the leaves and burn or dispose of them. That
prevents disease organisms and spores from overwintering on dead
leaves beneath the trees.

Mice enjoy nibbling on cherry trees, too. Clean cultivation several feet out from each tree is handy, although cherries will grow
well on lawns with just a little mulch around the trunks to avoid
bruising bark when you mow the grass.

harvesting

Knowing when to pick cherries is a precise art. As they mature
plump and ripe-looking, sample some. As soon as they seem sweet
enough or, in the case of sour ones, sweet enough to taste without
wincing or puckering your mouth, begin to pick. If you have used

nets, leave them on the trees until your harvest is over.

Cherries may take somewhat longer than other fruit trees to become established, but once they're rooted, cherry tarts, pies, jam and jelly can be made from your homegrown fruit for years to come.

10

n u t s

•

Nuts are actually fruits.
They just happen to be
the fruits of nut trees.
Once established and
nursed through their
traditionally slow start, nut
trees are about as carefree as
a tree can be. There's little
pruning needed and nearly
no other care.

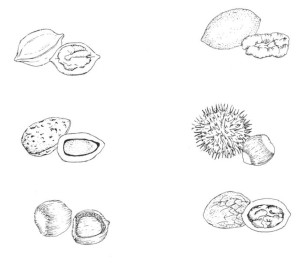

*Some of the tasty nuts you can grow in home gardens include from top left:
hickory, pecan; middle: almond and Chinese chestnut; bottom: hazelnut and walnut.*

Edible nuts are important horticultural crops in many sections of the United States. The value of almonds, filberts, pecans, and walnuts is well over $80 million annually.

Commercial growing is centered in the best climate areas, where soils are the most favorable. Pecans do well across the southern states, excluding Florida. They thrive in Georgia, Texas, and New Mexico, where the tree is a native.

Almonds and English walnuts are grown widely as commercial crops in California. Filberts are favored in Oregon and Washington.

However, nut trees grow surprisingly well outside these most favorable growing areas. By choosing the right types and varieties, you can grow nut trees in almost any state and in parts of Canada as well. In addition to being durable sources of shade, nut trees will reward you each fall with a tasty, rich harvest of nuts.

Most nut trees will require a companion for pollination. Check catalog listings so you can plan for two where cross-pollination by another variety of the same tree is required to produce the needed fruit set.

They are larger than most fruit trees and require a lot of room. Most nut trees have taproots—roots that grow long and deep down. That means you must dig in deeper and better to get them growing well. However, once that initial work is done, they can be remarkably hardy and long-lived. Some nuts are produced in bushes that may fit better in your landscape plans.

Here's a brief checklist of the most popular nut trees that can be grown and in which areas. They've been graded by a leading nursery, Henry Fields Seed and Nursery Company of Shenandoah, Iowa, a firm highly experienced with fruits and nuts since it was founded back in 1892.

America is divided into ten horticultural zones based on lowest average temperatures. A horticultural zone map is included in Appendix G of this book for ready reference.

Butternut trees yield rich, buttery-flavored nuts. They are usually hardy in zones 8 through 4. Trees may reach 40 to 60 feet tall. They are best planted in spring, about 30 feet apart. These tasty nut trees prefer rich soil, but otherwise no special care.

Chinese chestnuts have replaced American chestnut trees. A blight some years ago swept the nation, killing practically all our native chestnuts. Attempts are being made to bring back specially produced strains, but only time will tell whether these valiant efforts will succeed.

Chinese chestnuts are hardy from zones 8 through 4. These trees appreciate well-drained soil. They should be spaced 20 feet apart and prefer spring planting. Trees grow rapidly and bear early to provide you with large, sweet nuts. In shape, form, and size, the trees themselves resemble a standard apple tree not yet at its prime maturity.

Hazelnuts, called filberts in some areas, are another hardy landscape addition. The nuts are produced on vigorous shrubs that mature to about 6 feet tall. They are hardy in zones 8 through 2,

. . . .

which includes just about all but the most southerly and northerly portions of our country. As shrubs, they reward you with red and yellow foliage in the fall after you have harvested the nuts in late summer.

Hazelnuts prefer well-drained, rich soil and should be spaced 10 to 15 feet apart. They produce abundantly and nuts are cracked easily.

Hickory trees are native to America. These tall, hardy, pyramid-shaped trees prefer rich, well-drained soil. They are hardy in horticultural zones 8 through 4. If you keep them heavily mulched until they become established, they'll bear year after fruitful year. Hickory trees may reach 50 or more feet tall, so allow them ample growing room.

Pecans are more restricted in their habitat.They are hardy in zones 9 through 5, which does limit them to southern states. Pecans are large, spreading trees.They'll need 40 to 60 feet, measured in diameter, to reach their full potential. They prefer a deep soil with a steady moisture supply. Hardy pecans grow vigorously.

Pecans are handsome ornamental and shade trees well worth a spot in your plantscape for their attractive growth habit as well as for their nuts. Pecans respond to special cultivation, keeping soil tilled under the trees, and with this extra attention reward you more bountifully.

Walnuts are nicely rounded trees with deep green leaves. They are hardy from zones 8 through 4 and prefer rich loam where they can set strong roots. New varieties are nicely thin-shelled, which is a help at eating time. Plant them in the spring some 50 feet from each other and from other trees.

Filberts grow on a smaller nut-bearing bush or tree. They may reach 15 feet tall as trees, or only 8 feet high as bushes, depending on the type you buy. You can count on them for greater hardiness in northern areas. Filberts actually do best in colder areas rather than in the South. To ensure a crop, you must plant at least two for cross-pollination.

Because **filberts** are so attractive in many northern areas as a bush for home landscape use, you can shop for several improved varieties.

Italian red has a large, pointed nut with medium-thick shell. This tree is vigorous and one of the most productive of filberts.

Potomac is a vigorous hybrid between American and European varieties. It is hardy with attractive, somewhat rounded reddish brown nuts.

Walnuts, both black and hardy English types, are suitable for many areas too. The hardy English strains are often called **Carpathian** walnuts. They have superior tolerance to midwestern and northern winters; other English or Persian types may freeze back or be winter-killed.

Colby is a grafted variety of medium nut size. It cracks handily. Kernels are flavorful. Trees usually begin to bear in five to eight years and are very hardy.

Lake is another grafted variety that bears large, flavorful nuts. This tree, too, is hardy.

Among **black walnuts** that are native Americans, you'll find at nurseries some varieties adaptable to southern areas as well as northern climates.

Thomas is a grafted variety that bears early, producing good yields of thin-shelled nuts. It may be somewhat susceptible to leaf diseases.

Meyer is a grafted tree that bears early and produces fairly large yields of thin-shelled nuts. Nurseries offer seedling trees produced from outstanding native stock that produce satisfactory nuts. However, yields and quality are usually inferior to grafted varieties.

planting tips

Nut trees will reward you for many years, but they are notoriously slow to become established. They may seem to linger at the same size for several years before they take a firm roothold. Since most larger nut trees are mainly taprooted, rather than blessed with spreading roots, as most fruit trees are, you should pay special attention to the proper site. Choose an area that has the deepest soil possible. It should be well drained, have a rich and loamy type of soil, and receive abundant sun to help the tree produce its maximum yield.

Nurseries sell young saplings as well as older balled and burlapped nut trees. Younger ones, although slow to get started, are the best buy. Before your tree arrives, dig deeply in the spot you have selected.

Remember, taproots shouldn't be bent. They may look like a long, skinny parsnip, but from that root will grow your favored tree for many years to come. It deserves the best home you can provide. Dig down 3 feet, if possible. If subsoil is poor below the topsoil, remove it. Prepare a mixture of equal portions of compost and peat. Mix that with an equal quantity of topsoil.

As soon as your tree arrives, plant it. Set the root as deep as it needs to be. Add your improved soil mixture. Tamp it every few inches that you add. When the hole is half filled, soak the soil. Then add more soil until the hole is full. Soak again.

Leave a saucer-shaped depression as you would with a fruit tree. It is even more important to direct water to that taproot, since it can't reach out to search for moisture as easily as other trees can.

If the nut tree is small, stake it to give it the support it needs during the first few years on your land. Use rubber hose parts to protect the bark if you use wire to tie the tree to its stakes. Stout cord also may be used and shielded with old hose sections. You can also buy tree-staking kits with all the parts to keep the tree from bending in wind or during winter storms.

· ·

pruning pointers

If you can't bear to take those pruning shears to growing plants and trees, the next step may be the hardest. But prune you must to help that tree get off to the best possible start. Remove at least one-third to one-half of the top. It may sound severe, but it is to your tree's advantage. This pruning compensates for loss of root hairs and small rootlets from the main root when the tree is shipped and transplanted. Pruning also encourages that all-important new growth—the side branches that will become the framework of your mature nut-bearing tree.

By *not* pruning you risk formation of many small, weak sprouts that compete with each other. That first pruning, harsh as it may seem, is vital.

fertilizing

Mulching is my personal preference. A mulch around new trees preserves soil moisture that these taprooted nut trees need in order to start vigorous new growth. Mulch also reduces your temptation to mow grass too close to a tree planted on your lawn. By avoiding that problem, you won't bruise tender young bark.

Feeding young nut trees is a wise practice. You can mix liquid fertilizer solutions in water or use fertilizer sticks that you hammer into the ground around the tree. These slowly release plant nutrients to feed the tree as it needs more nourishment, month by month.

A handy tool is the Ross Root Feeder. It attaches to the end of a garden hose. Just drop a few tree-feeding pellets in its containers, turn on the faucet, and let the water dissolve the nutrients. They are carried into the soil with the water through the hollow spike that you insert easily in several spots around the tree.

Once your trees set their roots and begin feeding in their new home, your job is almost over. Check for any narrow crotches; they can split in winter storms. There's little need to worry about heavy crops weighing down the branches. These hardwoods can support abundant yields. Keep a lookout for damaged branches and limbs on older trees. Judicious pruning will prevent decay and deny insects a point of entry.

Most nut trees grow quite well as home-ground specimens or shade trees. Pecans, however, respond best to clean cultivation around them and fertilization. Since existing soil conditions and the requirements of varieties vary, it is best to check with your county agricultural agent for exact recommendations for your area.

With the increase in concern for our environment and the trend to return to more natural ways of life, families have found that wild nut trees require no tending to do their natural thing. You may find a nut tree or bush on your property when you move in. Many older homes were owned by people who saved the original nut trees they found when they built or bought the home. Or, with care, you can transplant some wildlings to your home grounds.

Here's a checklist of some native trees that you may find. If they aren't growing on your own land, always ask permission of the property owner if you wish to transplant any.

The **black walnut** is probably the best-known native American nut tree. It has hard, rough-textured bark and a tall, spreading growth pattern. Its round nuts are encased in a tough husk inside a softer greenish hull.

Nuts drop in the fall. They should be hulled as soon as the soft outer hull can be dented with your thumb. Wear gloves. The stain from the hull can discolor your hands. It also can discolor the nutmeats and give them an off flavor if you don't hull them promptly.

. . . .

After hulling, wash nuts with water and dry them on layers of absorbent paper. Place them in a shaded, cool, dry place with good air circulation for several weeks.

One way to remove tough, dark husks is to run over them with an automobile on a hard-surface driveway. That may sound strange, but it works. We've done it that way for years. A hammer works, too, but nuts tend to shatter.

Hickory nuts fall from those shaggy-barked hickory trees, called, not surprisingly, shagbark hickory trees and from other varieties of hickory trees. The small- to medium-size nuts are encased in hard, thin husks which can be cracked with nutcrackers without too much effort. Gather them as they fall, and dry them on screens. After a few weeks of drying, open a few to determine when the kernels inside are crisp. That's the time to store them. Store nuts in a mesh bag in a cool area with good air circulation.

Beechnut trees have smooth, light gray bark. Leaves turn brilliant yellow in the fall. Nuts are small and have sweet meat. The hard kernel is surrounded by a somewhat prickly husk. These, too, should be dried for a week or so on screens. You can crack them as you would the black walnuts. They are easier to crack if you soak them overnight in water.

If you prefer to crack and pick out the nutmeat from wild nuts, be sure to use it soon or dry it slightly on cookie sheets in a warm oven. Then, to store it for a few weeks longer, place it in tightly covered jars in the refrigerator or freezer. That helps prevent nut oils from becoming rancid.

Whether you plant domesticated nuts or gather some from the wild, remember that squirrels are just as quick to spot the time of harvest as you are. Keep an eye open for those furry rascals. They'll squirrel away a large part of your harvest if you don't get to picking first.

11

fruit-tree
sculpture—
the espalier

·

The horticultural

practice of espalier

(pronounced es-pal-

yay) is a centuries-old

tradition in France and

elsewhere in Europe.

Espalier means pruning

and training trees into

distinctive, sculptured shapes and patterns. It can be a most satisfying, creative, and attractive way to use trees and shrubs around your home grounds.

Results of espalier culture are dramatic. They can win you cheers from friends and neighbors as well as the real-estate broker when you may wish to sell your home.

The effects of espalier can be a daily pleasure for you as well. In addition, it offers an enjoyable challenge.

The practice was widely used by European gardeners in the Old World to conserve space in small orchards and on their home ground. Today the practice is making a striking comeback as a way to introduce decorative accents or conversation-piece plantings in home plantscapes.

An espalier is simply a living sculpture in your garden. It can brighten walls, fences, and property borders. A beautifully and cleverly trained plant is especially effective against a blank wall where close paving with driveway, path, or street prevents the use of a fully formed and naturally shaped plant.

In cities, driveways often take up a large share of the front yard, especially between homes on narrow-frontage lots. In such an area, one large espaliered tree can dramatically accent a garage or turn a neighboring wall that would otherwise be an eyesore into a fascinating display. One plant also is much less expensive than a large planting. And, despite its necessary periodic precise pruning, it requires less general care.

As you consider espalier, use the same judgment as you would in selecting specimen trees and shrubs. They should have enough room to provide the show for which they are intended without undue distraction.

Growing up a wall, espalier training provides both decorative landscaping and tasty fruit crops.

Espalier designs provide attractive living tree sculptures.

first steps

It is usually best to begin your espalier efforts with a young, un-trained tree. You can buy plants that have been given their first pruning for the espalier look in the nursery or at the garden center. There is, of course, usually a premium price on these pre-started specimens. It is just as easy to select a likely tree that has a sturdy young trunk and well-formed, nicely balanced branches that will respond to your careful pruning.

Most nurseries and garden centers have a reasonable selection of apple, pear, peach, and other suitable fruit trees and grapevines which lend themselves to successful espalier cultivation. Look for specimens that have sturdy, well-balanced limbs off the main trunk. Some shrubs and trees branch near the ground. They may not be suitable for regular use, but they can be just the right ones for your espalier plans.

Some trees that have been crowded in nurseries also may have somewhat flattened growth, with limbs already tending naturally in two directions and poor limbs elsewhere that can be removed to accentuate the flattened growth pattern. That's fine. If you ask for shrubs and trees for espalier use, you may find that they cost more. However, if you know what to look for, the comment that this flattened, poorer-looking tree might respond with your care, may make it yours for a lower price. Obviously, a flattened tree isn't the most desirable for use on a lawn or in a conventional landscape setting. Both you and the nursery win on such a deal.

Although branching on the young plant may not be perfect, make sure you get a healthy, sturdy tree or shrub. Some are grown in the nursery. Others are balled and burlapped, while others are container-grown. Be certain, as you would with trees for other parts of your grounds, that the bark is not damaged, that there are no broken main branches, and that there are no signs of insect or disease damage. It is possible to bring poor trees and shrubs back to health, but you are wiser to start off with healthy ones.

background considerations

Many materials can be used in developing an espalier support system. They can range from heavy-duty wire to wooden poles, from the reinforcing steel rods used in building construction to more elaborate trellises. Keep in mind that the design of your shrub or tree and its foliage is what you want to see, not the supporting materials.

As the young tree is being trained, the wires, poles, or other supports will be visible; but as the foliage fills in, even those supports that must be retained will be less obtrusive. Of course, you can paint supports to blend with the color of the wall or side of the background building. You also can paint them green, so they tend to vanish into the foliage of your living plants.

fruitful espaliers

Espaliered fruit trees provide a tasty extra attraction in your fruitful landscape. Especially useful when growing room is scarce, fruit trees and grapevines perform exceptionally well in espalier form.

You should select fruit trees grafted onto naturally dwarfing rootstock. They are designed for more unusual uses and won't range out of proportion. Semidwarf trees may be suitable for those large expanses, including hedgerow growing as property borders. However, dwarfing rootstock is probably your best bet.

You can choose whatever fruit you like best. Apple, pear, peach, quince, nectarine, crab apple, and even fig can be well trained into classic espalier shapes. Among these types you can usually find a number of favorite varieties.

With apples, for example, we have used dwarf varieties of **Northern Spy, McIntosh, Yellow** and **Red Delicious,** and **Lodi.** Local sources may offer different varieties that fit better into your climatic conditions. Dwarf pear trees also work well.

For truly limited space, dwarf peach trees are a delight. They grow only a few feet tall, but they can be shaped to delightful patterns.

the shapes to come

When it comes to creating espalier designs, let your imagination wander. You can create the classic branched candelabra.

Depending on the space you have, this can have three, four, five, or more branches. One Jewish friend even grew a menorah-shaped tree in honor of his faith. It became the hit of the year among the gardening friends of his temple.

You might try a checkerboard design or even a herringbone. For apples and even more appropriately for grapes, since it suits their natural growth habit, try a cordon espalier. The tick-tack-toe design is nicely distinctive as you train the trees to form a neat pattern of blocks and squares. This can be changed by proper pruning into a triangular pattern, more like the checkerboard style.

For an even more exotic shape, the Swedish Christmas tree has eye appeal to many. This type of espalier is more easily accomplished with vines and plants such as pyracantha than fruit trees. Yet, with patience and judicious pruning, you can create such highly personalized efforts with dwarf fruit trees.

The basic patterns shown in this chapter give you some idea of how to begin this periodic pruning in order to achieve espalier displays. As trees grow year by year, the simple pruning needed to maintain their shapes takes little time. A snipping in the fall when leaves are gone will realign the basic shape. Then summer pruning will keep side-branching under control.

Some gardeners believe that espalier pruning will cut into their fruit crop. It may, but not quite as much as you might imagine.

Remember that fruit trees respond naturally to pruning by compensating for the growth you cut away. They will surprise you with the abundance of bloom they set on new shoots. Remember, too, that by opening plants to sun and air, and reducing the number of fruits formed, you'll be rewarded with larger, healthier, easier-to-harvest crops.

Some patterns fit better in certain areas than others. The cordon design, for example, is effective against wide expanses of wall. It is attractive beneath high windows, especially on tall walls, because it provides a horizontal effect that helps bring the too-tall wall back into more pleasing perspective.

The simpler the design, the easier it will be to maintain. Study the background wall or area. Visualize which design will look best. Consider the background color of other foliage in adjacent properties and the need to paint and maintain walls behind your proposed espalier plants.

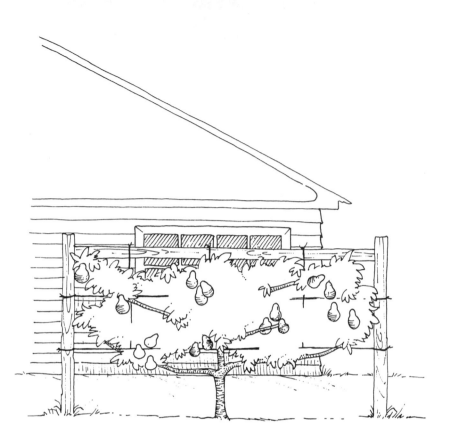

Trees trained in an espalier fashion, like this pear tree, may yield slightly less fruit, but can serve as a decorative accent and screen an unsightly area.

Try a sketch on paper first. Draw the background wall. Then trace the different designs to see which appeals most. Keep in mind windows that might be opened and power lines that may interfere as plants mature.

Although espalier is generally meant to grow in one plane, it is possible to train trees around a corner. By planting four trees in a square with a lattice roof, you can also create a coolly shaded sitting area. When the trees mature, their upper branches become your roof. Sitting beneath such a living garden arbor, we watched a friend reach up to pick an apple.

. . . .

planting and supporting espaliers

Plant your selected fruit trees as you would those intended for other parts of your home grounds. Dig the hole deep enough. Improve the soil by mixing humus, well-rotted manure, peat, or compost with the soil in whatever proportions are needed.

Before you plant, plan and erect your espalier supports. Reinforcing steel rods used in construction or sturdy posts to which you anchor training cables or heavy wires should be positioned well. Some of them can be removed later, when your trees take proper and desired shape. Don't set them in concrete. They will be needed for only a few years.

The simplest design to create is a fan or hand. You can secure rods, posts, or poles at least a foot, perhaps 18 inches, deep in the soil. Be sure to keep them away from the wall since you do need room to prune behind as well as among the branches of your chosen plants.

If you use wires, take up the slack so they don't sag and whip around in the wind. Loose wire can whip into tender bark, cutting and scarring it, resulting in damage spots that disease and insects can penetrate.

Once the basic support is in place, plant your tree, shrub, or vine. When it is planted firmly, attach the limbs to the support with short lengths of soft twine or weather-resistant wire coated with paper or plastic. (Uncoated wire will cut into bark and girdle stems too easily. However, wire run through plastic fish-tank hose or similar material serves well.)

Branches can be bent a bit to achieve the desired effect. But heed this caution: *don't* try to accomplish complete shaping all at once! Branches may be flexible, but they will break if bent too far. Give them time to turn naturally in your proposed direction. In another 4 to 6 weeks, bend and tie again, leading them in your preferred pattern step by growing step.

Once you have attached the desired branches to their supports, step back and examine your progress. Plants don't grow perfectly in balance, so don't be disappointed. A bit of careful pruning of growth here, an unwanted minor branch there, will let you mold your living sculpture to your own desires.

If your espalier is placed against a wood or even a brick wall, you can possibly do without a freestanding support. Eye hooks or J-hooks can be screwed to the wall at appropriate points. Limbs and branches can be tied to them, not too tightly nor too loosely. Ice storms do occur in some areas and can break branches on your espaliers if you don't leave them enough room to sway with winds.

When you must maintain the wall, painting or touching up cement, the connecting cord or coated wire can be loosened. Then pull the espalier plant over gently and tie to a stake until the paint is dry.

Special nails can be driven into the mortar of brick or concrete walls. A soft lead tongue is attached to the head of these nails and bent over to secure the branch.

You can also establish your espalier on a frame of heavy wire such as modern plastic-coated clothesline. If the white color offends your aesthetic sensibilities, paint it green to blend in with the foliage.

pruning pointers

Once you have your frame in place and your espalier planted well and secured to it, think about the shapes to come. Keep pruning shears handy, but don't be too hasty. Once you cut away a branch or branchlet, seldom will another sprout there, but you encourage others to form elsewhere.

Watch for branchlets that grow parallel to the ground and for those that grow toward or away from the wall. They will spoil the espalier look quickly if you don't remove them.

The best time to prune is when flower buds form. Then you can see where future blooms and fruits or berries will be and avoid cutting them away. Each side or "lateral" shoot that forms along the main stem should be removed at the main stem if it is not part of your desired pattern.

When new growth appears in unwanted places, pinch off or clip away the tip to prevent stray branchlets from growing. With a little practice, you'll soon get the feel of plantscaping to the living sculpture forms you want.

Root pruning is often overlooked. Many espaliered trees and shrubs grow vigorously and can outgrow even your dedicated pruning effort. Root pruning checks growth and also encourages flowering and fruiting.

To prune the roots, simply dig a shallow trench around the tree about 2 feet away from the trunk. It will cut away some large, thick roots. Do this judiciously, since you only want to keep the plant in check, not destroy too much of its food- and water-gathering root system. Sometimes you can root-prune by spading around low-growing espalier shrubs.

Fertilize your espaliered fruit trees somewhat less than you would if they were left to grow to their natural full size; about half the usual amount of fertilizer. Tips for feeding fruit trees are included in the appropriate chapters of this book. Deep-root feeding with fertilizer spikes placed in hand-driven holes around the trunks, or root-feeding devices like the Ross Root Feeding tool used with a garden hose, can give espalier plants a boost in season.

The nicest part about espaliered trees and shrubs is that once you have established them, just minimal pruning each year keeps them in bounds. For little care, they'll give you back lots of pleasure that is distinctively your own creation.

12

pest~control guidelines

•

Insect enemies and

plant diseases can

attack even the best-

tended fruit trees and

bushes. Although it's

true that healthy,

vigorous plants have

some ability to

withstand and fight off

disease and insect problems, at times a combination of conditions favors the pests and not your plants.

Before that time comes, it helps to know some of the archvillains that may visit your home fruit planting. If you can spot these problems and pests before they launch full-scale attacks, they are easier to defeat.

Prevention of problems before they occur has its obvious advantages. Chemical sprays, whether or not you approve of them, can prevent most insect and disease problems. There are ways to select the better, safer-to-use materials that stop pests yet have few, if any, adverse effects on people or the environment.

recognizing pests

Here's the rogues' gallery. Being able to identify them will help you to banish them before they eat your fruitful harvests.

Aphids (plant lice) attack foliage of many types of fruits. These small, soft-bodied insects suck juice from leaves, causing them to crinkle or curl. Aphids are usually green, brown, or black.

Cankerworms and other loopers feed on the leaves and young fruits of many trees. When disturbed, they drop and hang suspended on strands of silk. They usually disappear by late spring or early summer.

Codling moths are responsible for wormy apples and pears. The larvae eat through the flesh of apples, leaving tunnels filled with brown debris.

Cyclamen mites are tiny pests. They live in the crown of strawberry plants and attack leaves and flower buds. Leaves become wrinkled and brown at the tips. Mites may prevent fruit formation or cause misshapen fruit.

Fall webworms develop in large web nests on the branches of fruit trees during late summer or fall. They eat leaves in and around the nest. Prune off branches and destroy the nests by burning as soon as they appear.

Grasshoppers often strip trees of foliage and tender bark. When hoppers become numerous, control them in ground cover and fence rows to prevent them from migrating to fruit trees. If hoppers hit fruit trees, ask your garden center for the appropriate spray.

Leafhoppers are green, gray, or tan, about ⅛ inch long. They feed on the undersides of leaves of many fruits. Young hoppers suck juice from leaves. They may transmit diseases from one tree to another.

Lesser peach-tree borers attack stone-fruit tree trunks and scaffold branches, particularly where pruning wounds and other injuries make penetration easy. Look for a gummy exudate.

Peach tree borers work at the base of stone-fruit trees. Sawdust castings and gummy masses at the base of the trunk indicate their presence.

Plum curculios are snout beetles. They deposit eggs in young tree fruits. Egg punctures are crescent-shaped rather than round, as with the plum gouger. Damaged fruit generally turns red prematurely and falls from the tree.

Plum gougers are another type of snout beetle. They deposit eggs in stone fruits while the fruits are small. Larvae burrow into the pit and emerge as adults, leaving a matchstick-size hole in the fruit. Try this: Spread a canvas in early morning under the infested tree. Strike the trunk with a padded mallet or shake it vigorously. Destroy all beetles that drop onto the canvas. Repeat at four-day intervals until no more beetles are found.

Scale insects are small sucking insects about ⅒ inch long. Except for a brief period when the young are hatched, scale insects remain attached to a branch or twig. **Oystershell scale** is brownish and has a shape similar to that of an oyster shell. **Scurfy scale** is white and pear-shaped.

Spider mites are tiny insectlike pests that suck juices from leaves, which eventually become bronzed and dried and fall. They are frequently troublesome during dry years. Their presence may be detected by fine webs on the undersides of leaves. Hosing trees with water from a garden hose often aids in control.

See Appendix A for a tree-by-tree listing.

recognizing damaging diseases

Diseases can sometimes cause as much damage as insects do. Severe diseases can defoliate trees and cause the dropping of most of the fruit. Here's a list of the most common. If you spot them early, you can apply necessary fungicides to control the problem.

Apple scab is a fungus that infects the leaves, twigs, and fruit of apple trees. This disease appears on leaves as dark green velvety spots. On fruit, it first appears as a slightly raised brown or black round spot that later breaks open to form a scab. Infected fruits frequently crack or become malformed. Fungi overwinter in fallen leaves and infect trees again during rainy weather in spring.

Keep trees well pruned so that sunlight and wind will dry the leaves quickly after rain. Also clean up around the trees and, where permitted, burn leaves.

Brown rot of stone fruits is primarily a fruit disease, but it also infects leaves, flowers, and twigs, giving them a frosted look. If ripening fruit is infected, brown spots will form and enlarge until the entire fruit becomes soft, watery, and discolored. Fruits later become covered with brown tufts, dry up, and hang like mummies on the tree. They should be removed and burned because the disease overwinters in them.

Cedar rust, often called apple rust or cedar apple rust, is a fungus that originates on cedar trees and infects apple trees. On cedar trees the disease appears as a corky brown gall. During spring rains, galls swell to become an orange-colored, jellylike mass, which contains spores that infect fruit trees.

On apple trees this disease appears first as yellow spots on the upper leaf surface. These spots increase in size and become orange with small black specks in the centers. Leaf tissue beneath spots swells into blisters with tubular projections. Severe infections may cause leaf drop and deformed fruit. If possible, remove red cedar trees from within a ¼-mile radius of your apple trees.

Fire blight is a bacterial disease that may severely injure susceptible varieties of apples and pears. Pollinating insects transmit the disease to blossoms, and sucking insects transmit it to growing shoots. The disease normally starts in growing tips and progresses downward, killing all tissue it invades. Infected leaves become brown or black, dry up, and remain attached to branches.

Infected twigs become dark, their bark is sunken. A milky or brownish ooze may form on the infection. Cankers form where the disease enters a large branch or trunk. The bacteria overwinter in these cankers and are a source of infection the following year.

As soon as you notice diseased shoots, remove them by breaking or cutting them off several inches below the infection. If a cutting tool is used, it must be disinfected in strong household bleach—*after every cut*—so that bacteria will not be spread to healthy tissue.

Remove suckers and water sprouts that grow from the trunk and large branches, since these sprouts are highly susceptible to blight. Disease readily passes through them into older wood.

Plum pockets is a fungus disease that infects the fruits, shoots, and leaves of plums. Infected fruits and shoots puff up into large hollow masses and eventually drop.

Powdery mildew infects many plants and is occasionally serious on cherries. It causes a white moldy growth that distorts leaves and stem tips.

Sunscald is a winter injury rather than a disease. In late winter or early spring, the bright afternoon sun warms the southwest side of trees and activates cells under the bark. These cells are then killed by later freezing. Bark sloughs off, leaving a canker that will weaken and eventually kill the tree. Sunscald usually injures the trunk and large limbs.

It can be prevented by several methods of protection. You can lean boards over the southwest side of the tree to shade it from the sun, wrap the tree trunk with burlap, tar paper, or aluminum foil, or whitewash the trunk and large limbs to reflect the sun. Natural-color tree wrapping is available at garden centers; it is unobtrusive and works well.

Knowing when to spray or dust is important in controlling harmful insects and plant diseases on your fruit trees. Proper timing will help you solve the problems and provide adequate protection for the plants between treatments.

Some areas have more insect problems than others, and sometimes different types of pests. Seasons are different, too. One year you may have lots of rain, which requires more attention to "cover" sprays to prevent mildews, spots, and rusts on trees and fruit bushes or vines. If you have just sprayed and you get heavy rains, you may need to spray again after the rain to reapply the material that has washed off the foliage, leaving it unprotected.

Every county agricultural agent has a suggested spray schedule that has been tested in his or her area and state. Your best bet is to check with your agent for the timing, recommended materials, and success rates of the chemicals proven most effective on your state's approved list.

Some states have much more restrictive rules governing which pesticides may be applied. As newer, improved pesticides are becoming available, it is best to always check with your county agricultural agent or other appropriate local adviser before beginning your pest-control schedule.

Organic or natural gardeners avoid any use of chemical pesticides and rely on alternative methods that prove effective.

You can write your county agricultural extension office for listings of organic gardening suppliers and make your own decisions on which system you prefer.

On our own fruit trees, we prefer to strike a reasonable balance. If we find especially severe disease or insect problems, we resort to the methods recommended by our state agricultural experts and used by commercial fruit growers. However, the decision of which approach to adopt is your personal choice. It should be governed, of course, by your proximity to other properties with pets and children.

The following guide will provide the general procedure for when and how often you should plan to protect your fruit crops from damage by insects and plant diseases. You may prefer different materials. Consult your local pesticide supplier for details about the materials that have proved most effective in the specific climate, soil, and other conditions of your area, and which are approved for use in your state.

We have found these general guidelines most useful in plotting our campaign of pest control and prevention.

apples and pears

DORMANT SPRAY

For scale, aphids, and red mites, use a dormant or miscible spray oil. Apply in spring before green begins to show in buds.

DELAYED DORMANT SPRAY

For apple scab and mildew, use microfine wettable sulfur. Apply when unfolding leaves are ¼ to ½ inch long.

PRE-BLOOM SPRAY FOR APPLES (May be omitted on pears)

For apple scab and mildew, use microfine wettable sulfur. Apply when most of the blossom buds are beginning to show color and the individual buds have separated into clusters.

BLOOM SPRAY

For scab, mildew, and cedar rust, use microfine wettable sulfur or recommended fungicide. Apply when about one-quarter of the blossoms are open.

PETAL FALL SPRAY

For scab, cedar rust, codling moth, curculio, and leafrollers, use recommended fungicide plus recommended insecticide. Apply after most of the petals have fallen.

FIRST COVER SPRAY

For scab, cedar rust, codling moth, curculio, and leafrollers, use the same materials as for petal fall spray, above. Apply about seven to ten days after the petal fall spray.

SECOND COVER SPRAY

For scab, cedar rust, codling moth, curculio, and leafrollers, use recommended fungicide and pesticide. Apply about seven to ten days after the first cover spray.

THIRD, FOURTH, AND FIFTH COVER SPRAYS

For scab, codling moth, leafrollers, and mites, use recommended fungicide. Apply at intervals of seven to ten days.

SUMMER COVER SPRAYS

For scab, summer diseases, codling moth, leafrollers, and mites, use recommended fungicide and insecticide. We generally use Sevin (carbaryl) or malathion because we believe they are safer to use and provide reasonably broad-spectrum pest control. Check label directions, of course, for the insects that each controls.

The number of cover sprays needed will depend on the maturity date of the variety. Summer cover sprays may be applied at intervals of ten to fourteen days. DO NOT apply certain pesticides or combinations on apples or pears within seven days of harvest. Read label details on nearness of applications to harvest and follow manufacturer directions precisely.

peaches, plums, and apricots
(Avoid sulfur on Apricots)

DORMANT SPRAY

For scale insects and peach leaf curl, use a dormant spray every year. Use dormant or miscible spray oil plus recommended fungicide. Apply early in the spring, shortly before any growth begins. Mix the spray oil and fungicide together before adding water. Shake or stir vigorously, then add a small quantity of water and stir again, after which the combination should mix with the remainder of the water.

PRE-BLOOM SPRAY

For brown rot and insects, use microfine wettable sulfur plus recommended insecticide. Apply when blossom buds show pink.

BLOOM SPRAY

For brown rot, use microfine wettable sulfur. Apply when about a quarter of the blossoms are open.

PETAL FALL SPRAY

For brown rot, scab, and curculio, use microfine wettable sulfur plus recommended insecticide. Apply when most of the petals have fallen.

SHUCK SPRAY

For brown rot, scab, curculio, and Oriental fruit moth, use the same material as for petal fall spray. Apply about ten days after petal fall spray.

FIRST, SECOND, AND THIRD COVER SPRAYS

For brown rot, scab, curculio, and Oriental fruit moth, use microfine wettable sulfur plus recommended insecticide. Apply about ten days after shuck spray and at ten-day intervals.

SUMMER COVER SPRAYS

For brown rot, Oriental fruit moth, and mites, use recommended fungicide and insecticide. The number of cover sprays needed will depend on the maturity date of the variety. Apply summer sprays at ten- to fourteen-day intervals. **DO NOT** use pesticide combinations within two weeks of harvest.

PREHARVEST SPRAYS

For brown rot and mites, use recommended fungicide. If mites are present, add recommended insecticide, but not within seven days of harvest unless approved by label directions. Apply one spray about two weeks before harvest and a second spray about one week before harvest.

SPECIAL SUMMER SPRAYS

For peach borer, use recommended insecticide. Make three applications: (1) the first week of June; (2) the first week of July; (3) the first week of August. **DO NOT** use within the number of days of harvest as indicated on the label of the material being used. Apply as a spray or with a brush to the trunks of the trees from the ground line up to about one foot on the trunk. Permit the material to run down the trunk and soak into the ground.

cherries

DORMANT SPRAY

For overwintering pests and scales, use dormant or miscible spray oil. Apply in the spring before any green is showing in the buds.

PETAL FALL SPRAY

For mildew, leaf spot, brown rot, and curculio, use recommended fungicide and insecticide. Spray when most of the petals have fallen.

FIRST COVER SPRAY

For mildew, leaf spot, brown rot, and curculio, use the same materials suggested for petal fall spray. Apply ten days after petal fall
spray.

SECOND COVER SPRAY

For mildew, leaf spot, brown rot, and curculio, use recommended fungicide and insecticide. Apply about ten to twelve days
after the first cover spray.

AFTER-HARVEST SPRAY

For mildew and leaf spot, use recommended fungicide and insecticide. Apply as soon as all the fruit has been picked. During
wet summers, apply a second after-harvest spray about three to
four weeks later.

appendix a
common threats
to fruits

•

Here's a summary of pests, organized by their fruit-tree preference. Insect guides and literature from pesticide manufacturers provide close-up details about these insect enemies so you can identify them and learn how to eliminate them.

insects that attack small fruit trees

Apple	codling moth, curculio, tent caterpillar, cankerworm, apple maggot, European red mite
Apricot, Peach, Nectarine	plum curculio, peach borer, Oriental fruit moth
Cherry	plum curculio, tent caterpillar, cherry maggot
Pear	plum curculio, pear psylla, codling moth
Plum	plum curculio

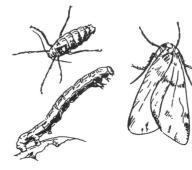

Fall Cankerworm

Length: 1¼ inch
Male moth, wingless female. Larvae feed on fruit and other trees. Cankerworm is a similar species.

Pistol Casebearer

Length: ½ inch
Brown worm enclosed in curved, silken case. Eats holes in leaves and buds and in fruits of apple, pear, cherry, and plum trees.

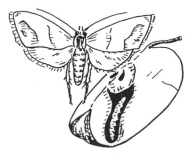

Red-banded Leaf Roller

Length: ¾ inch
Early larvae roll leaves and spin slight webs. The later generations attack fruit.

Codling Moth

Length: ¾ inch
The major apple tree pest. Larvae feed on fruit until fully grown.

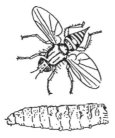

Cherry Fruit Fly

Length: ⅙ inch
Yellow and black fly. Larvae develop inside fruit,
leaving no outside evidence until nearly fully grown.

Apple Maggot/Railroad Worm

Length: ¼ inch
Dark brown to yellowish-white adult. Maggots make
irregular winding tunnels in fruit

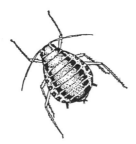

European Peach Aphid

Length: 1/12 inch
The major pest of peach trees in some areas, this insect
sucks sap from fruit, leaves, and twigs.

San Jose Scale

Length: 1/12 inch
Yellow, moist-appearing, circular insect concealed be-
neath scale. Disfigures fruit and can kill trees.

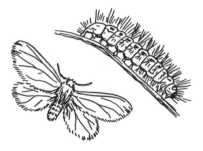

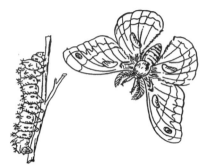

Fall Webworm

Length: 1¼ inch
Pale-yellow, black-spotted hairy caterpillar that feeds in dirty white, loosely-woven web on tree leaves.

Cecropia Moth

Length: ⁶/₇ inch
Pale-green, red, and yellow larvae feed on foliage of apple and other fruit trees, as well as shrubs.

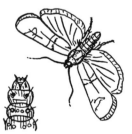

Apple Leaf Skeltonizer

Length: ½ inch
Dark-green, active caterpillars cause late-summer/early-fall injury to trees by feeding in a web.

Oriental Fruit Moth

Length: ⅜ inch
Attacks peach, apple, and other fruit trees. Early larvae tunnel twigs, and later ones feed in fruit.

Wooly Apple Aphid

Length: 1/10 inch
*Attacks aerial parts and roots of tree. Can cause
serious gall-like swellings on roots. Prefers apple but
will attack other trees.*

Pear Pyslla

Length: 1/10 inch
*Sucks sap from foliage and other tree parts, which
weakens tree and discolors fruit.*

Yellow-necked Caterpillar

Length: 2 inches
Moth larvae feed on foliage of orchard and walnut trees.

Red-humped Caterpillar

Length: 1 1/4 inch
*Larvae has a striking appearance and can sometimes
defoliate apple and other nursery trees.*

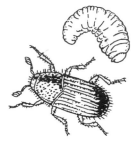

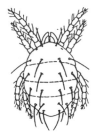

Peach Bark Beetle

Length: ¹⁄₁₀ inch
Resembles shot-hole borer. Larvae tunnel across grain
of wood.

European Red Mite

Length: ¹⁄₅₀ inch
Attacks apple, pear, peach, and plum trees. Discolors
foliage, and can cause defoliation.

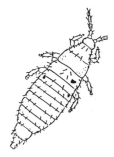

Pear-Slug

Length: ¹⁄₅ inch
Sluglike larvae of black sawfly. Feeds on leaves of
pears, cherries, plum, apples, and other plants.

Pear Thrips

Length: ¹⁄₁₂ inch
Dark, yellowish-brown insect that feeds on fruits and blossoms
and on the leaves of peach, plum, and apple trees.

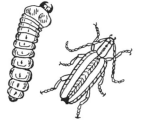

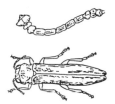

Roundheaded Apple Tree Borer

Length: ¾ inch
Larvae bore into tree and feed on sapwood and heartwood.

Sinuate Pear Tree Borer

Length: ⅓ inch
Bronz adult feeds on foliage. Flat-headed larvae work under bark, boring galleries.

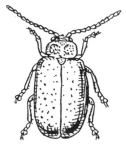

Plum Curculio

Length: ¼ inch
Feeds on stone fruits and apples. Adult feeds on fruit and foliage. Grub feeds inside fruit.

Cherry Leaf Beetle

Length: ¼ inch
Red beetle that attacks plum and apple foliage. Larvae feed only on wild cherry.

appendix b
basic guide
to thinning

•

Thinning is necessary to ensure that trees put their growing strength into a selected amount of properly sized fruits. That way, these fruits become plumper, juicier, and tastier. Too many fruits left on trees to mature will result in smaller, less-desirable fruits come harvesttime. Here's a guide for hand-thinning to let your trees produce the best possible fruit. Remove fruits to the distance suggested along each branch.

Apple	6 to 8 inches
Apricot, Peach, Nectarine	2 to 3 inches
Cherry	1 inch
Pear	4 to 5 inches
Plum	1 inch for small
	2 to 3 inches for large

appendix c
basic spacing guide
for home fruit trees

•

Here's a handy guide to distances between rows and individual plants in home mini-orchards. If you interplant with other landscape trees and shrubs it works about as well.

Fruit	Distance In Feet Between Rows / Plants		Usual Bearing Age	Approximate Yield And Period
Apple	20–25	35	6–8 yrs.	3–6 bushels, Aug.–Oct.
Dwarf Apple	15–20	8–10	4–5 yrs.	2 bushels, Aug.–Oct.
Dwarf Pear	15–20	10–20	3–4 yrs.	1 bushel, Aug.–Sept.
Peach, Apricot, Nectarine	15–20	20	3–4 yrs.	2 bushels, July–Sept.
Plum	15–20	20	4–5 yrs.	1 bushel, Aug.–Sept.
Cherry, sweet	20–25	25	6–7 yrs.	1 bushel, July
Cherry, sour	15–20	20	4–5 yrs.	1 bushel, July

appendix d
quantities for
freezing, canning,
and making jams,
jellies, and preserves

•

This book is not intended as a guide to freezing, canning, or making jams, jellies, or preserves. However, since many gardeners like to know what quantities of different types of fruit convert to quantities for their home freezer or for estimating yields for other uses, here's a list I've used for years. It varies, naturally, with size of fruit, state of ripeness, and variety. However, it gives you a guide to planning for ways to preserve the fruits of your gardening fun.

Fruit	Amount	Yield
Apple	1 bushel	32–40 pints
	1¼ lbs.	1 pint
Cherry	1 bushel	36–44 pints
	1¼ lbs.	1 pint
Peach, Apricot, Nectarine	1 bushel	32–48 pints
	1–1½ lbs.	1 pint
Pear	1 bushel	40–50 pints
	1–1¼ lbs.	1 pint
Plum	1 bushel	38–50 pints
	1–1½ lbs.	1 pint

appendix e
where to get help
in your state

•

Every state has a land-grant agricultural college as part of its state university system. At these colleges you can consult a variety of horticultural specialists, from landscape experts to pomologists who serve the citizens of their state.

In addition, the Cooperative Extension Service of each state is a federally and state funded organization that can be highly valuable to you as you plan and plant your fruitful landscape. State Extension specialists are charged with the responsibility of providing information to homeowners and residents of their states.

In addition, each county in the United States has county extension specialists. These people also are well trained in providing detailed information about fruit trees, berry bushes and plants, home planting, and horticulture in general. Since space does not permit listing all the county extension agents, I'm providing the addresses of the colleges and universities. Address your inquiries to:

Agricultural Information Office
College of Agriculture

From them you can get the names and local addresses of the county specialists.

In general, the county specialists are at the county seat of government in each of the thousands of counties across America. In effect, an army of talented and dedicated people is available to assist you in many ways, from soil testing to advising on the best varieties of trees and shrubs, bushes, and plants that will perform best under your own local climate, soil, and other growing conditions.

Auburn University
Auburn, AL 36830

University of Alaska
College, AK 99708

University of Arizona
Tucson, AZ 85721

University of Arkansas at
Little Rock
Little Rock, AR 72204

University of California
at Berkeley
Berkeley, CA 94720

Colorado State University
Fort Collins, CO 80521

University of Connecticut
Storrs, CT 06268

University of Delaware
Newark, DE 19716

Federal Extension Service
U.S. Department of Agriculture
Washington, D.C. 20250

University of Florida
Gainesville, FL 32601

University of Georgia
Athens, GA 30602

University of Hawaii
Honolulu, HI 96822

University of Idaho
Moscow, ID 83843

College of Agriculture
University of Illinois
Urbana, IL 61801

Purdue University
West Lafayette, IN 47907

Iowa State University
Ames, IA 50010

Kansas State University
Manhattan, KS 66502

University of Kentucky
Lexington, KY 40506

Louisiana State University
Baton Rouge, LA 70803

University of Maine
Orono, ME 04473

University of Maryland
College Park, MD 20742

. . . .

University of Massachusetts
Amherst, MA 01003

Michigan State University
East Lansing, MI 48824

University of Minnesota
Minneapolis, MN 55455

Mississippi State University
State College, MS 39762

Agricultural Building
University of Missouri
Columbia, MO 65211

Montana State University
Bozeman, MT 59717

College of Agriculture
University of Nebraska
Lincoln, NE 68588

University of Nevada
Reno, NV 89507

University of New Hampshire
Durham, NH 03824

Rutgers, The State University
of New Jersey
New Brunswick, NJ 08903

New Mexico State University
Las Cruces, NM 88003

Cornell University
Ithaca, NY 14850

North Carolina State University
Raleigh, NC 27695

North Dakota State University
Fargo, ND 58105

The Ohio State University
Columbus, OH 43210

Oklahoma State University
Stillwater, OK 74078

Oregon State University
Corvallis, OR 97331

The Pennsylvania State
University
University Park, PA 16802

University of Puerto Rico
Rio Piedras, PR 00928

University of Rhode Island
Kingston, RI 02881

Clemson University
Clemson, SC 29634

South Dakota State University
Brookings, SD 57007

University of Tennessee
Knoxville, TN 37901

Texas A & M University
College Station, TX 77843

Utah State University
Logan, UT 84321

· ·

University of Vermont
Burlington, VT 05405

West Virginia University
Morgantown, WV 26506

Virginia Polytechnic Institute
Blacksburg, VA 24061

University of Wisconsin
Madison, WI 53706

Washington State University
Pullman, WA 99163

University of Wyoming
Laramie, WY 82071

appendix f
for more
information about
fruit growing . . .

•

Your best bet for additional information about fruit growing in specific areas is the agricultural extension office in states known for major fruit-producing regions.

Here are the major states in fruit growing. Address your inquiries for bulletins to the agricultural extension service director. If you live elsewhere, you can expect to pay a slight charge for mailing to an out-of-state resident.

University of Illinois
Urbana, IL 61801

University of Massachusetts
Amherst, MA 02002

Michigan State University
East Lansing, MI 48823

Rutgers University
The State University of
    New Jersey
New Brunswick, NJ 08903

New York State Agricultural
    Experiment Station
Geneva, NY 14456

New York State College of
    Agriculture and Life Sciences
Ithaca, NY 14850

Ohio State University
Columbus, OH 43210

And, of course, check with your own state extension service. Missouri, California, and Georgia all have exceptional literature on specific aspects of home growing. (See Appendix E for addresses.)

appendix g

•

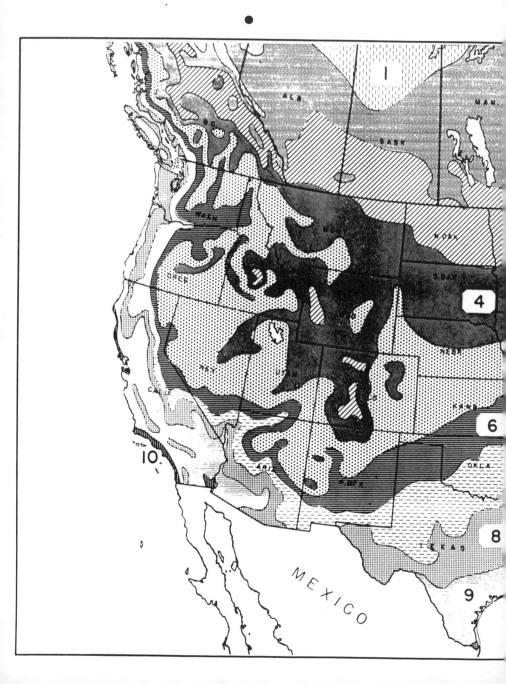

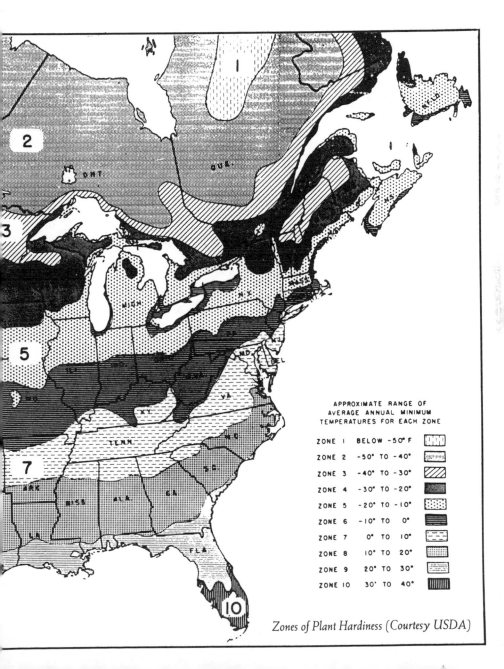

APPROXIMATE RANGE OF
AVERAGE ANNUAL MINIMUM
TEMPERATURES FOR EACH ZONE

ZONE 1   BELOW -50° F
ZONE 2   -50° TO -40°
ZONE 3   -40° TO -30°
ZONE 4   -30° TO -20°
ZONE 5   -20° TO -10°
ZONE 6   -10° TO   0°
ZONE 7   0° TO 10°
ZONE 8   10° TO 20°
ZONE 9   20° TO 30°
ZONE 10   30° TO 40°

Zones of Plant Hardiness (Courtesy USDA)

appendix h
mail-order
nurseries that offer
fruit and nut trees

•

Bear Creek Nursery
P.O. Box 411
Northport, WA 99157

Burpee Seeds
300 Park Ave.
Warminster, PA 18991

Chestnut Hill Nursery
Rt 1, Box 341
Alachua, FL 32615

Fruit Growers Co-op
New York State
  Experiment Station
Geneva, NY 14456

Gurney Seed & Nursery
10 Capital Street
Yankton, SD 57078

McFayden
P.O. Box 1030
Minot, ND 58702-1030

Miller Nurseries
5060 West Lake Rd.
Canandaigua, NY 14424

Park Seed Co.
Cokesbury Rd.
Greenwood, SC 29647-0001

Spring Hill Nurseries
110 West Elm Street
Tipp City, OH 45371

Stark Bro's Nurseries
Louisiana, MO 63353

index

•